DINOSAUR
NUMBER CRUNCH!

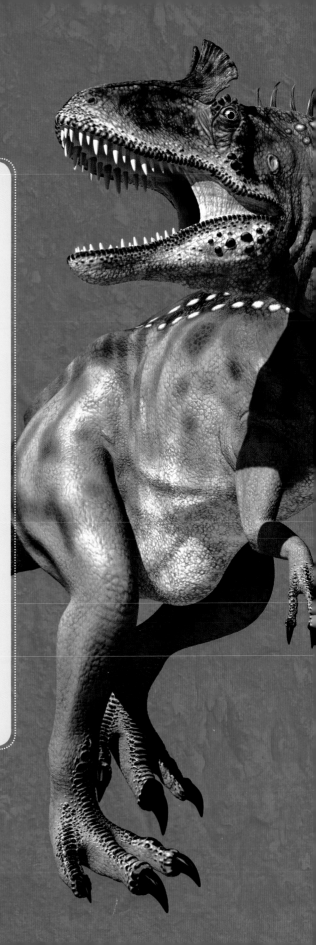

THIS IS A CARLTON BOOK

Published in 2018 by Carlton Books Limited,
an imprint of the Carlton Publishing Group,
20 Mortimer Street, London W1T 3JW

Author: **Kevin Pettman**
Design and illustration: **WildPixel LTD.**
Executive Editor: **Jo Casey and Stephanie Stahl**
Managing Art Editor: **Dani Lurie**

A catalogue record for this book is available from
the British Library.

ISBN: 978-1-78312-363-6

Printed in China

10 9 8 7 6 5 4 3 2 1

DINOSAUR
NUMBER CRUNCH!

THE FIGURES, FACTS AND PREHISTORIC
STATS YOU NEED TO KNOW

KEVIN PETTMAN

CARLTON
KiDS

CONTENTS

DINOSAUR NUMBER CRUNCH

In this book you will find giant sauropods like Argentinosaurus and Brachiosaurus, mini monsters such as Anchiornis and Archaeopteryx, and everything else in between. This is your ultimate guide to more than **200** dinosaurs – with a few ancient reptiles lurking around as well!

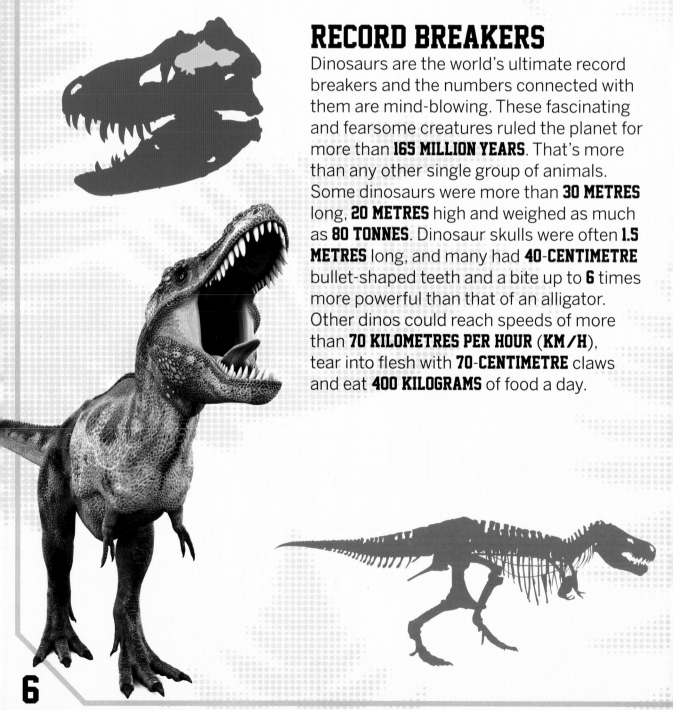

RECORD BREAKERS

Dinosaurs are the world's ultimate record breakers and the numbers connected with them are mind-blowing. These fascinating and fearsome creatures ruled the planet for more than **165 MILLION YEARS**. That's more than any other single group of animals. Some dinosaurs were more than **30 METRES** long, **20 METRES** high and weighed as much as **80 TONNES**. Dinosaur skulls were often **1.5 METRES** long, and many had **40-CENTIMETRE** bullet-shaped teeth and a bite up to **6** times more powerful than that of an alligator. Other dinos could reach speeds of more than **70 KILOMETRES PER HOUR (KM/H)**, tear into flesh with **70-CENTIMETRE** claws and eat **400 KILOGRAMS** of food a day.

GET TO THE CRUNCH

Don't think you need to be as brainy as the super-smart Stenonychosaurus to understand all these facts, figures and stats! Each piece of information is written in bite-sized chunks and illustrated with an easy graphic that even a Stegosaurus would understand. By the way, did you know that despite measuring **7 METRES** and weighing **3 TONNES**, Stegosaurus had a brain **25** times smaller than that of a human? Turn the pages to discover loads more brain busters!

BATTLE IT OUT

You will also learn about the most amazing dinosaur battles. You'll see deadly killers like Tyrannosaurus rex scrap with Spinosaurus; Argentinosaurus face off with Amphicoelias and the famous Triceratops take on Velociraptor. These duels never actually happened in the dinosaur world, but pitching them against each other in this book reveals all sorts of numbers and information about the most spectacular species ever to roam planet Earth.

YEAR WE GO...

The first numbers you'll discover will tell you exactly when dinosaurs appeared, how long they ruled for, the different periods they lived through and when they disappeared from the planet.

Mesozoic era = Between **252** and **65 MYA** (million years ago)
Triassic period = **252** to **201 MYA**
Jurassic period = **201** to **145 MYA**
Cretaceous period = **145** to **66 MYA**

530 MYA

Invertebrates (animals without backbones) and later vertebrates (animals with backbones) grew rapidly in numbers. Reptiles and **4**-legged vertebrates were common between about **300** and **252 MYA**.

Sauropods

Coelophysis

232 MYA

Dinosaurs began to evolve (develop).
The first dinos to evolve were small,
2-legged creatures, such as Coelophysis.

200 MYA

Sauropods – heavy dinosaurs with long necks and tails – emerged at the end of the Triassic period and grew to huge sizes in the Jurassic.

200 MYA

At the start of the Jurassic period, dinosaurs had adapted to the changing climate and conditions of the planet and were the dominant land animals. Birds began to evolve around this time.

145 MYA

During the Triassic period, all of the planet's landmasses were joined together, forming one huge supercontinent, called Pangaea. By the Cretaceous period, Pangaea had split into smaller continents. Dinosaurs adapted to their new surroundings and more species evolved.

NUMBER CRUNCH

Early in their development, dinosaurs may have split into **2** orders (families). The saurischians, which included sauropods and the theropods, and the ornithischians, which included stegosaurs, ankylosaurs and other sub-orders.

Tyrannosaurus rex

Triceratops

70 MYA

Tyrannosaurus rex, probably the most famous and well-known dinosaur of all time, appeared about **68 MYA**.

66 MYA

The dinosaurs (except birds) died out. Their mass extinction was caused by a huge **11-KILOMETRE**-wide asteroid suddenly striking Earth. About **85 PER CENT** of all living things were wiped out.

66 MYA TO PRESENT

Birds and some land and sea reptiles survived the mass extinction. They lived into the Cenozoic era, which is what we're living in now.

4 MYA

Humans begin to evolve from the hominid mammals, who first appeared in Africa.

TEN THINGS YOU PROBABLY DIDN'T KNOW ABOUT DINOSAURS

From bones and brainpower to stones and slow movers, check out these **10** dino facts you should know.

100

1. Dinosaurs reigned for **165 MILLION YEARS**, but at times there were just a few species roaming the planet. Between **83** and **70 MILLION YEARS** ago, around **100** types existed. This is known as the golden age of dinosaurs.

Quetzalcoatlus

2. The animals that existed at the same time as dinosaurs, like Quetzalcoatlus and its **11-METRE** wingspan, were types of flying reptile, but not really dinosaurs.

3. Humans actually lived nearer to the time of the mighty Tyrannosaurus rex than some other dinosaurs did. T. rex died out **66 MILLION YEARS** ago, but the huge Amphicoelias, for example, perished **145 MILLION YEARS** ago.

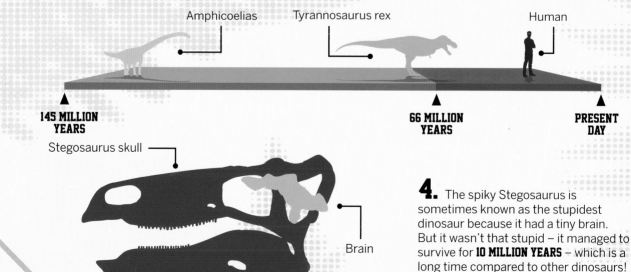

Amphicoelias

Tyrannosaurus rex

Human

145 MILLION YEARS

66 MILLION YEARS

PRESENT DAY

Stegosaurus skull

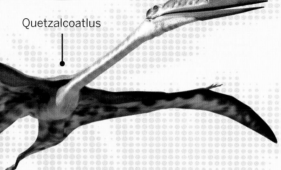

Brain

4. The spiky Stegosaurus is sometimes known as the stupidest dinosaur because it had a tiny brain. But it wasn't that stupid – it managed to survive for **10 MILLION YEARS** – which is a long time compared to other dinosaurs!

5. Most big dinosaurs were slow movers, and the **30-TONNE** Diplodocus was no exception. However, it did have a super-fast tail that it may have swiped at attackers at over **1000 KM/H**. That's a supersonic speed!

Diplodocus

Tyrannosaurus rex

6. T. rex was pretty fierce, and its arms were quite strong but rather short – they were less than **1 METRE**.

7. When dinosaur remains were first found in China over **3,000 YEARS** ago, people thought they were the bones of mythical dragons.

8. The meat-eating Herrerasaurus was one of the first dinosaurs to use its claws to grab, injure or kill prey, about **230 MILLION YEARS** ago.

Herrerasaurus

Sauroposeidon

9. Not many dinosaur bones have been found in the huge country of Australia. Less than **10** skeletons have been discovered in Queensland and just **6** bones in the vast state of Western Australia.

Queensland

Western Australia

10. Some dinosaurs, like the **40-TONNE** Sauroposeidon, may have swallowed stones to help mash up the rough plants and vegetation in their stomachs.

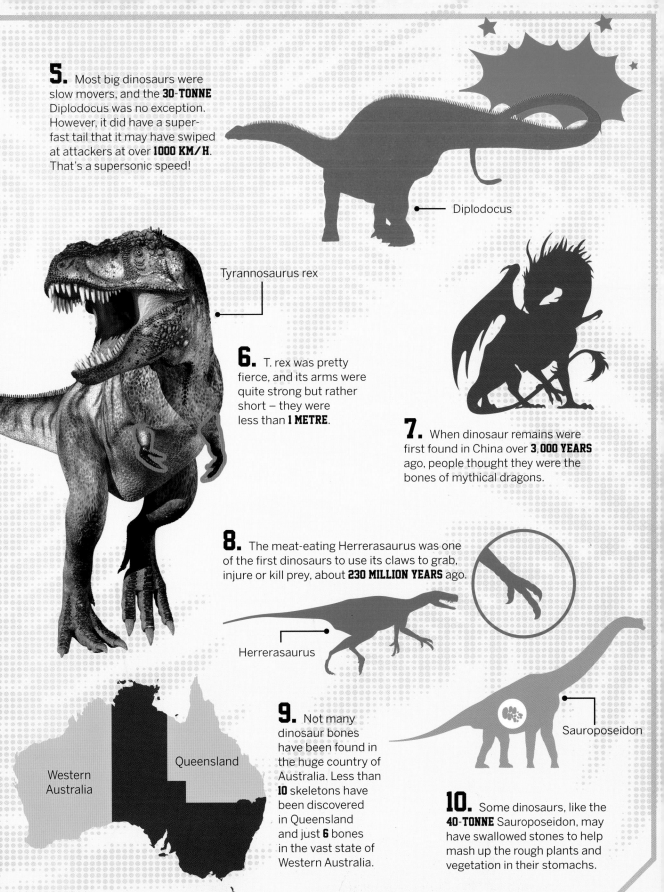

DEADLY KILLERS

Are you ready to meet some serious killing machines? These are the most deadly, dangerous and destructive creatures ever to roam planet Earth!

Tyrannosaurus rex

Scary killer Tyrannosaurus rex hunted at least **2** types of large dinosaurs – Triceratops and Edmontosaurus.

Triceratops

Edmontosaurus

30 CM

Liopleurodon

The giant sea killer Liopleurodon grew to lengths of up to **15 METRES**. Its banana-shaped teeth could grow to **30 CENTIMETRES** – that's the length of a school ruler.

Anchiornis claw

At a tiny **40 CENTIMETRES**, the Anchiornis is the smallest predator dinosaur ever discovered. It weighed just **250 GRAMS**, which is about the same as **5** packets of crisps.

40 CM

Anchiornis hunted lizards with the **3**-clawed fingers on each of its wings. Although it had long feathers, it couldn't fly. It simply glided short distances.

6 METRES

300
YEARS

Megalosaurus was discovered more than **300 YEARS** ago in England and was the first dinosaur to be acknowledged by scientists.

Megalosaurus

It was about **6 METRES** long with powerful arms. It used its **3**-clawed feet to hunt plant-eating dinosaurs.

Herrarasaurus

NUMBER CRUNCH
Giganotosaurus had a mighty
1.6-METRE-long skull
– which is the height of
2 washing machines.

Giganotosaurus

4.5 METRES

At **4.5 METRES** long, Herrarasaurus was the first big meat-eating dino that lived, about **250 MILLION YEARS** ago. That's **150 MILLION YEARS** before Tyrannosaurus rex.

THOUSANDS of fossil remains of the meat-eating Coelophysis were found at Ghost Ranch, New Mexico, in **1947**. These small and speedy predators died together in the largest dinosaur grave ever discovered.

Coelophysis

Giganotosaurus used its **8-TONNE** weight to take down prey. It also hunted bigger sauropods, sometimes hunting for up to **2 HOURS** before launching a ferocious ambush.

Saltwater crocodile

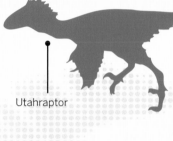

7 METRES

The deadly Utahraptor was **7 METRES** long, but only weighed about **700 KILOGRAMS**, which is about the same dimensions as a large saltwater crocodile.

Utahraptor

Deinonychus

Deinonychus weighed the same as a small adult human – about **60 KILOGRAMS** – and hunted larger prey in packs of **5-10.** It was super fast and could reach speeds of up to **50 KM/H.**

30 KM/H
(Average speed of a human)

50 KM/H

Triceratops

Triceratops was a large plant eater – at **9 METRES** it was the size of a bus. It attacked with its **3** sharp horns when it felt threatened.

9 METRES

5 FRIGHTFULLY LARGE HUNTING DINOSAURS

1. Spinosaurus	18 METRES LONG / 10 TONNES
2. Carcharodontosaurus	13 METRES LONG / 7 TONNES
3. Giganotosaurus	12.5 METRES LONG / 8 TONNES
4. Tyrannosaurus rex	12 METRES LONG / 6 TONNES
5. Mapusaurus	12 METRES LONG / 6 TONNES

1ST

Velociraptor was a medium-sized predator that lived **71-75 MILLION YEARS** ago. Its secret weapon was a deadly **9-CENTIMETRE** curved claw on the **SECOND** toe of each foot, which it used like a knife to stab prey.

NUMBER CRUNCH
Velociraptor was feathered, fast and fearless. It could reach speeds of up to **40 KM/H.**

$8.36 MILLION

That's how much the remains of a Tyrannosaurus rex sold for at an auction in the USA in **1990**.

Albertosaurus

At **9 METRES** and **1.5 TONNES**, Albertosaurus was smaller and more aerodynamic than its cousin, Tyrannosaurus rex. It could chase, hunt and kill prey very successfully.

9 METRES

The remains of **26** Albertosaurus were found in one area of Alberta, Canada, in **1910**.

Alberta

CLASH OF THE KILLERS

They lived millions of years apart and in different parts of the world, but these two killers were the kings of their territories.

NAME: TYRANNOSAURUS REX

SUPER-SIZED STATS
Weight: **6 TONNES**
Length: **12 METRES**
Height: **6 METRES**
Top speed: **32 KM/H**
Location: **NORTH AMERICA**
Lived: **67–65 MILLION YEARS AGO**

x 6 = T. rex bite

Experts think Tyrannosaurus rex had one of the strongest bites ever. It was **6 TIMES** stronger than an alligator's snap!

Spinosaurus was more powerful than a T. rex and had **3** knife-like claws on each hand. The thumb claw was a deadly cutting weapon.

NAME: SPINOSAURUS

SUPER-SIZED STATS
Weight: **10 TONNES**
Length: **18 METRES**
Height: **7 METRES**
Top speed: **32 KM/H**
Location: **NORTH AFRICA**
Lived: **112–95 MILLION YEARS AGO**

NUMBER CRUNCH
Tyrannosaurus rex and Spinosaurus lived **TENS OF MILLIONS** of years apart.

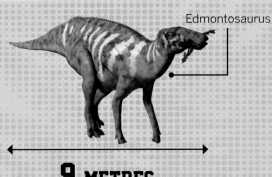
Edmontosaurus

9 METRES

The deadly Tyrannosaurus rex was known to attack the giant Edmontosaurus, which was **9 METRES** long and weighed the same as an African elephant.

Tyrannosaurus rex had small, muscular arms, each with **2** ultra-sharp claws to slash flesh.

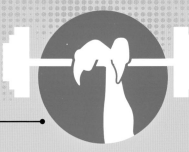

T. rex had about **50** razor-sharp teeth. It could take up to **2 YEARS** for new teeth to grow.

They were up to **40 CENTIMETRES** long, including the root. That's longer than the length of your elbow to the tip of your finger!

24 HRS

Experts think Tyrannosaurus rex could hunt any time of night or day. That means it was a **24-HOUR** nightmare for the dinosaurs it hunted!

3 METRES

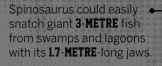

The huge spines on its back were up to **2 METRES** long, which is as tall as a door. The ferocious-looking spines helped control body temperature, attract a mate and scare off rivals.

Spinosaurus probably fought with another giant predator, Carcharodontosaurus. This beast was **13 METRES** long and weighed **7 TONNES**. These deadly rivals used their mighty teeth and claws to rip and stab each other.

Spinosaurus could easily snatch giant **3-METRE** fish from swamps and lagoons with its **1.7-METRE**-long jaws.

Spinosaurus hunted on land and in the sea, making it the most all-round killing machine to walk, or wade, across the planet.

HIGH AND MIGHTY

These long and tall creatures have set many records in the dinosaur world. Check out these brilliantly big stats and facts.

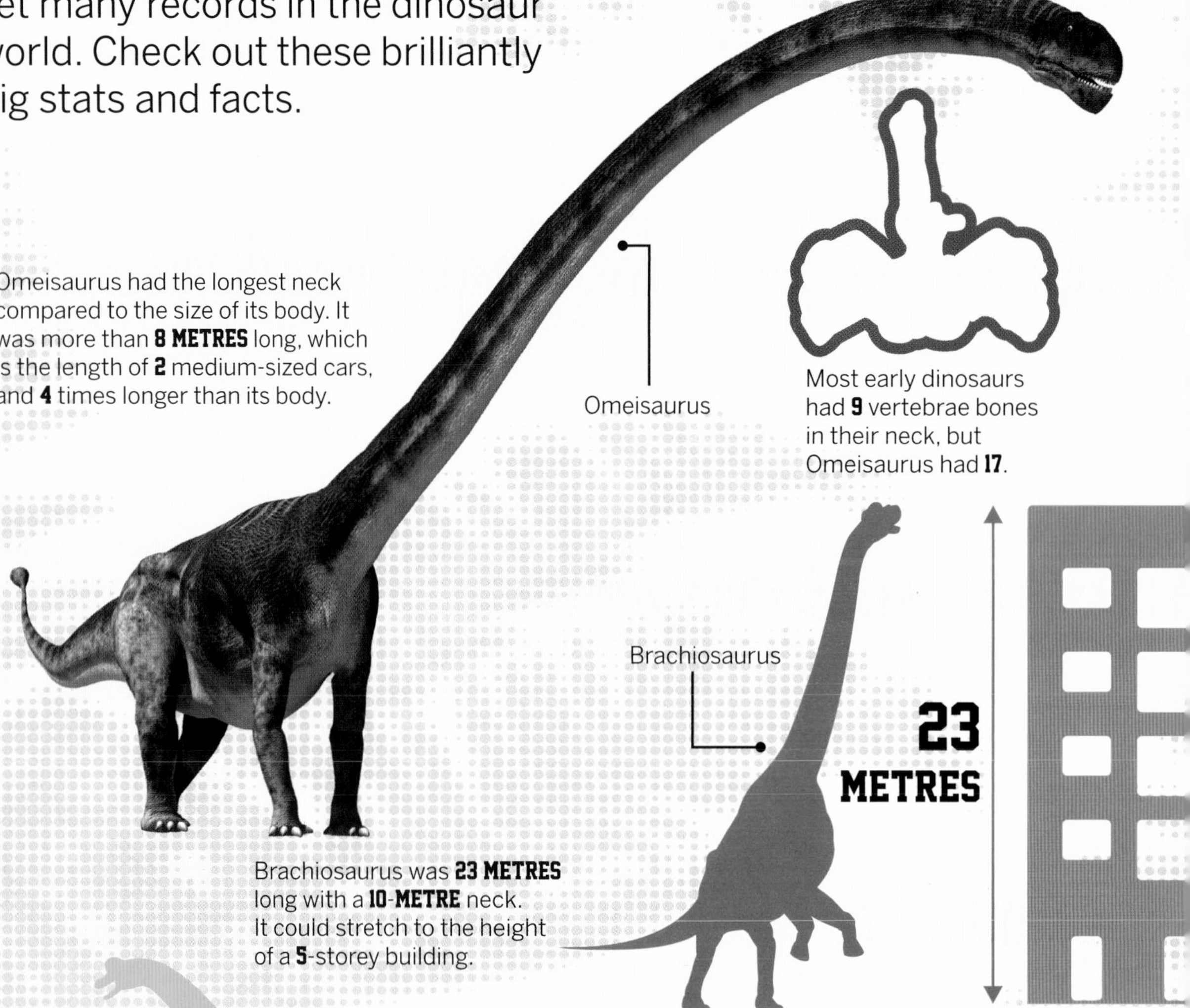

Omeisaurus had the longest neck compared to the size of its body. It was more than **8 METRES** long, which is the length of **2** medium-sized cars, and **4** times longer than its body.

Omeisaurus

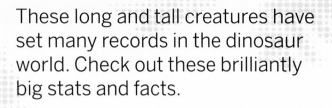

Most early dinosaurs had **9** vertebrae bones in their neck, but Omeisaurus had **17**.

Brachiosaurus

23 METRES

Brachiosaurus was **23 METRES** long with a **10-METRE** neck. It could stretch to the height of a **5**-storey building.

Its front legs were longer than its back legs, with upper leg bones more than **1.5 METRES** long.

1.5 METRES

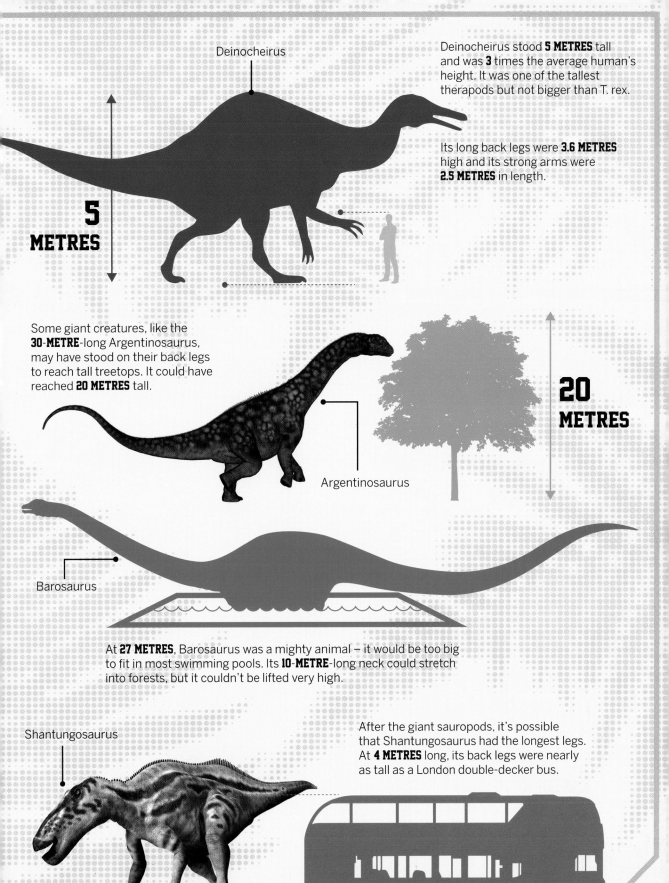

Deinocheirus

Deinocheirus stood **5 METRES** tall and was **3** times the average human's height. It was one of the tallest therapods but not bigger than T. rex.

Its long back legs were **3.6 METRES** high and its strong arms were **2.5 METRES** in length.

5 METRES

Some giant creatures, like the **30-METRE**-long Argentinosaurus, may have stood on their back legs to reach tall treetops. It could have reached **20 METRES** tall.

Argentinosaurus

20 METRES

Barosaurus

At **27 METRES**, Barosaurus was a mighty animal – it would be too big to fit in most swimming pools. Its **10-METRE**-long neck could stretch into forests, but it couldn't be lifted very high.

Shantungosaurus

After the giant sauropods, it's possible that Shantungosaurus had the longest legs. At **4 METRES** long, its back legs were nearly as tall as a London double-decker bus.

TALE OF THE TALLEST

It's time to get your tape measure out – these two tall and long creatures tower over any other land animal. Make sure you don't get in their way!

NAME: DIPLODOCUS

SUPER-SIZED STATS
Weight: **30 TONNES**
Length: **32 METRES**
Height: **ABOUT 7 METRES**
Top speed: **16 KM/H**
Location: **USA**
Lived: **150–147 MILLION YEARS AGO**

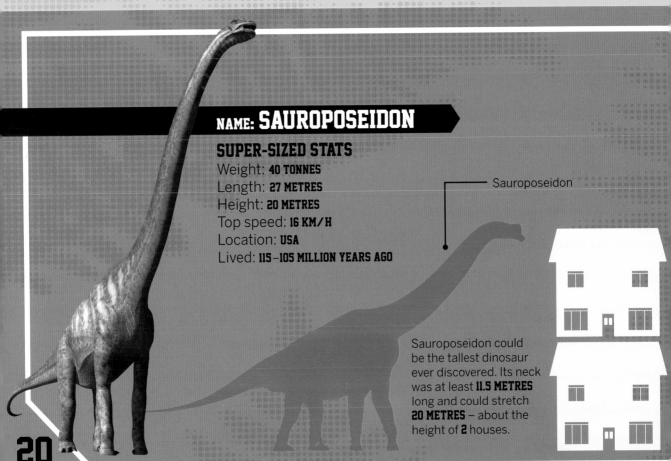

NAME: SAUROPOSEIDON

SUPER-SIZED STATS
Weight: **40 TONNES**
Length: **27 METRES**
Height: **20 METRES**
Top speed: **16 KM/H**
Location: **USA**
Lived: **115–105 MILLION YEARS AGO**

Sauroposeidon

Sauroposeidon could be the tallest dinosaur ever discovered. Its neck was at least **11.5 METRES** long and could stretch **20 METRES** – about the height of **2** houses.

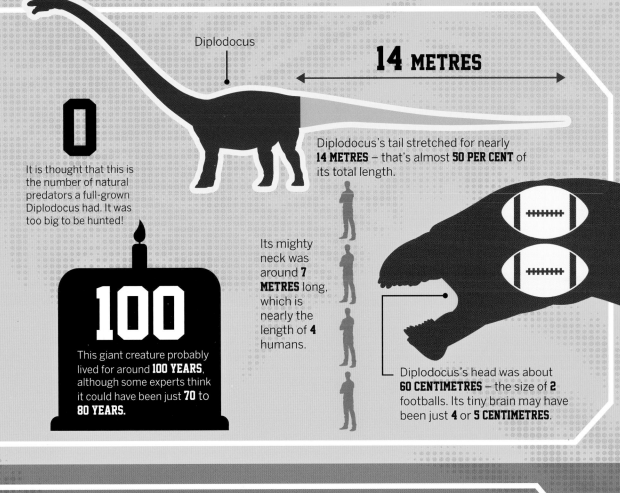

Diplodocus

14 METRES

Diplodocus's tail stretched for nearly **14 METRES** – that's almost **50 PER CENT** of its total length.

0

It is thought that this is the number of natural predators a full-grown Diplodocus had. It was too big to be hunted!

100

This giant creature probably lived for around **100 YEARS**, although some experts think it could have been just **70** to **80 YEARS**.

Its mighty neck was around **7 METRES** long, which is nearly the length of **4** humans.

Diplodocus's head was about **60 CENTIMETRES** – the size of **2** footballs. Its tiny brain may have been just **4** or **5 CENTIMETRES**.

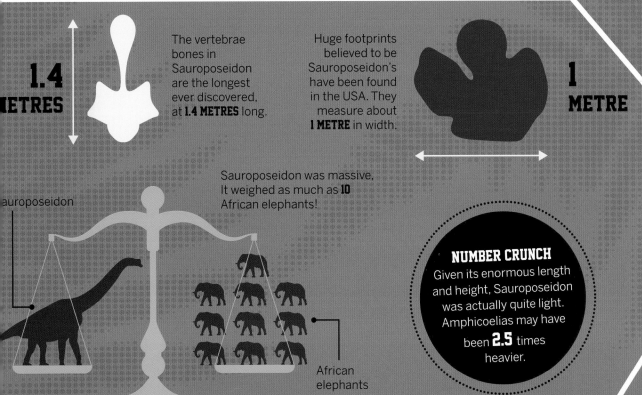

1.4 METRES

The vertebrae bones in Sauroposeidon are the longest ever discovered, at **1.4 METRES** long.

Huge footprints believed to be Sauroposeidon's have been found in the USA. They measure about **1 METRE** in width.

1 METRE

Sauroposeidon was massive, It weighed as much as **10** African elephants!

Sauroposeidon

African elephants

NUMBER CRUNCH

Given its enormous length and height, Sauroposeidon was actually quite light. Amphicoelias may have been **2.5** times heavier.

SUPER HEAVYWEIGHTS

These colossal creatures would break any bathroom scales! Discover heavyweight facts about Amphicoelias, Apatosaurus, Shantungosaurus and more...

Only **2** bones from the huge Amphicoelias dinosaur have been found, but it's thought to be the heaviest dinosaur ever, weighing up to **100 TONNES**.

Amphicoelias

Some giant plant-eating sauropods, like Sauroposeidon and Camarasaurus, weren't as heavy as other dinos because their long necks had large hollow spaces.

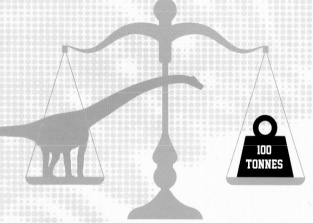

100 TONNES

Shantungosaurus

15 TONNES

One of the largest non-sauropods was the duckbilled Shantungosaurus. It was **15 TONNES** and even on all fours its head was **4 METRES** off the ground. It had **HUNDREDS** of back teeth for grinding plants and even trees.

5 HUGE AND HEAVY DINOSAURS

1. Amphicoelias   **UP TO 100 TONNES**
2. Argentinosaurus   **70–80 TONNES**
3. Sauroposeidon   **40–50 TONNES**
4. Brachiosaurus   **35 TONNES**
5. Diplodocus   **30 TONNES**

Sauropods had to walk on all **4** legs to support their massive weight.

Brachiosaurus

x4

1/10

Isanosaurus lived about **210 MILLION YEARS** ago and was one of the earliest sauropods. It weighed **3 TONNES**, which is just **10 PER CENT** of a Diplodocus's weight.

Hypselosaurus egg

x73

Hypselosaurus was a **7-TONNE** titanosaur that laid eggs **73** times bigger than chicken eggs.

Chicken egg

100+

Some experts think that titanosaurs roamed most of the Earth's continents in herds of **100** or more.

The armoured Ankylosaurus weighed **6 TONNES**. Its thigh muscles were **6** times bigger than a human's, at about **3.5 METRES**.

The **20-TONNE** Apatosaurus was a plant eater and it's possible that it ate more than **100 KILOGRAMES** of plants each day. That's the same weight as an average giant panda.

Apatosaurus

HUNDREDS of huge Apatosaurus footprints can be seen near Purgatoire River, Colorado, USA.

BATTLE OF THE BIGGEST

Two of the heaviest, longest and mightiest dinosaurs go head to head in a battle of the big beasts!

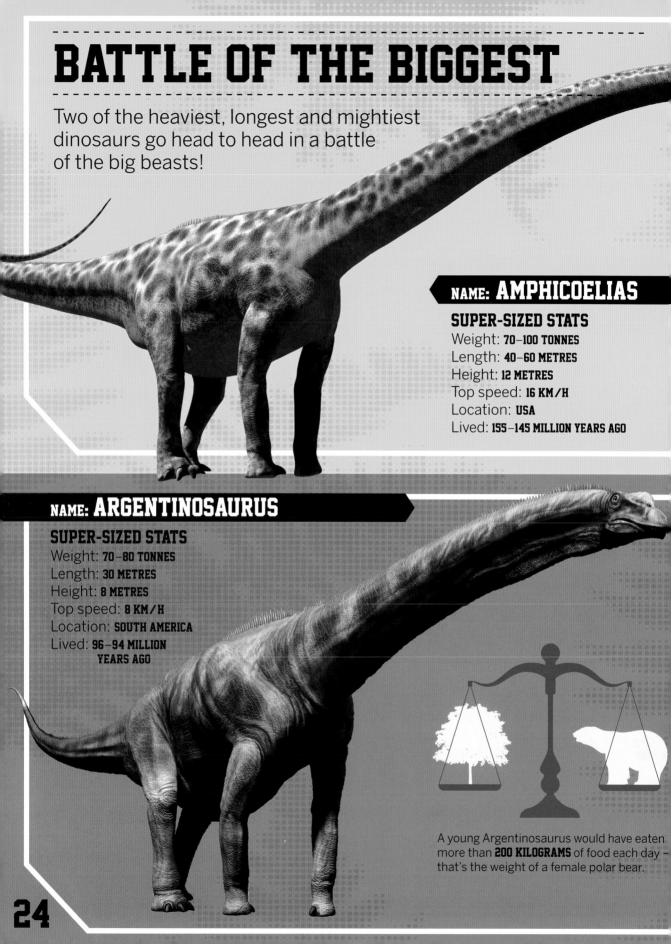

NAME: **AMPHICOELIAS**

SUPER-SIZED STATS
Weight: **70–100 TONNES**
Length: **40–60 METRES**
Height: **12 METRES**
Top speed: **16 KM/H**
Location: **USA**
Lived: **155–145 MILLION YEARS AGO**

NAME: **ARGENTINOSAURUS**

SUPER-SIZED STATS
Weight: **70–80 TONNES**
Length: **30 METRES**
Height: **8 METRES**
Top speed: **8 KM/H**
Location: **SOUTH AMERICA**
Lived: **96–94 MILLION YEARS AGO**

A young Argentinosaurus would have eaten more than **200 KILOGRAMS** of food each day – that's the weight of a female polar bear.

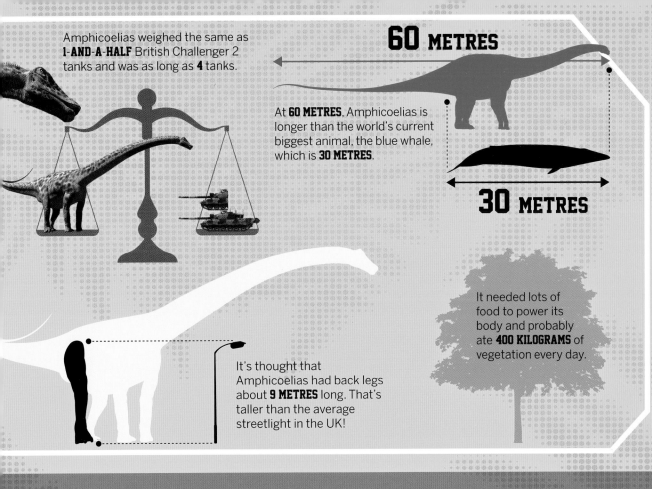

Amphicoelias weighed the same as **1-AND-A-HALF** British Challenger 2 tanks and was as long as **4** tanks.

60 METRES

At **60 METRES**, Amphicoelias is longer than the world's current biggest animal, the blue whale, which is **30 METRES**.

30 METRES

It needed lots of food to power its body and probably ate **400 KILOGRAMS** of vegetation every day.

It's thought that Amphicoelias had back legs about **9 METRES** long. That's taller than the average streetlight in the UK!

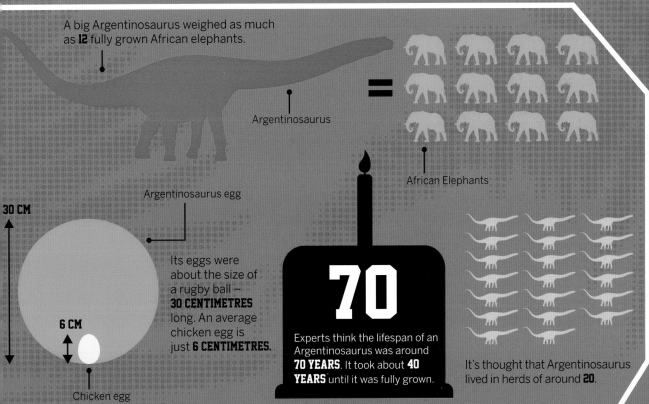

A big Argentinosaurus weighed as much as **12** fully grown African elephants.

Argentinosaurus

=

African Elephants

30 CM

Argentinosaurus egg

Its eggs were about the size of a rugby ball – **30 CENTIMETRES** long. An average chicken egg is just **6 CENTIMETRES**.

6 CM

Chicken egg

70

Experts think the lifespan of an Argentinosaurus was around **70 YEARS**. It took about **40 YEARS** until it was fully grown.

It's thought that Argentinosaurus lived in herds of around **20**.

TINY TERRORS

In the dinosaur world, small didn't mean cute and cuddly – these tiny terrors would give anyone a BIG fright!

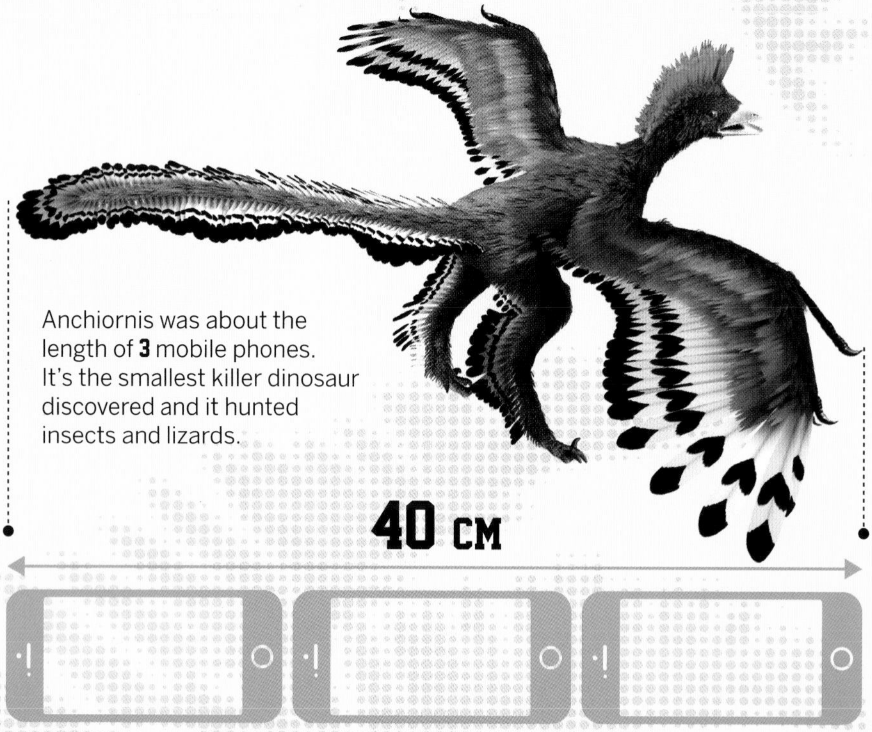

Anchiornis was about the length of **3** mobile phones. It's the smallest killer dinosaur discovered and it hunted insects and lizards.

40 CM

Anchiornis

Pigeon

NUMBER CRUNCH
Anchiornis was small, but speedy! It was a bird-like dinosaur that could probably reach speeds of up to **30 KM/H.**

Anchiornis weighed about the same as a pigeon. The massive killer Spinosaurus was **40,000** times heavier.

TOP 5 DINKY DINOS

1. Anchiornis	**40 CM**
2. Parvicursor	**45 CM**
3. Caenagnathasia	**45 CM**
4. Mei long	**45 CM**
5. Mahakala	**50 CM**

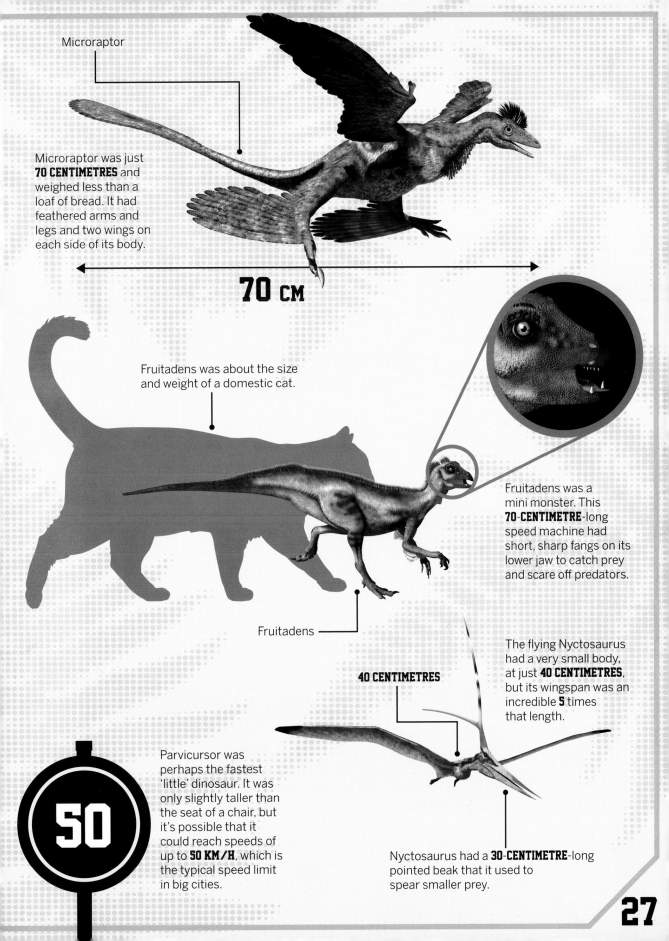

Microraptor

Microraptor was just **70 CENTIMETRES** and weighed less than a loaf of bread. It had feathered arms and legs and two wings on each side of its body.

70 CM

Fruitadens was about the size and weight of a domestic cat.

Fruitadens was a mini monster. This **70-CENTIMETRE**-long speed machine had short, sharp fangs on its lower jaw to catch prey and scare off predators.

Fruitadens

40 CENTIMETRES

The flying Nyctosaurus had a very small body, at just **40 CENTIMETRES**, but its wingspan was an incredible **5** times that length.

Parvicursor was perhaps the fastest 'little' dinosaur. It was only slightly taller than the seat of a chair, but it's possible that it could reach speeds of up to **50 KM/H**, which is the typical speed limit in big cities.

50

Nyctosaurus had a **30-CENTIMETRE**-long pointed beak that it used to spear smaller prey.

27

MORE TINY TERRORS

Remains of tiny terrors like Parvicursor and Mei long have been found in China and Mongolia, more than **10,000 KILOMETRES** from the giant sauropods of North and South America.

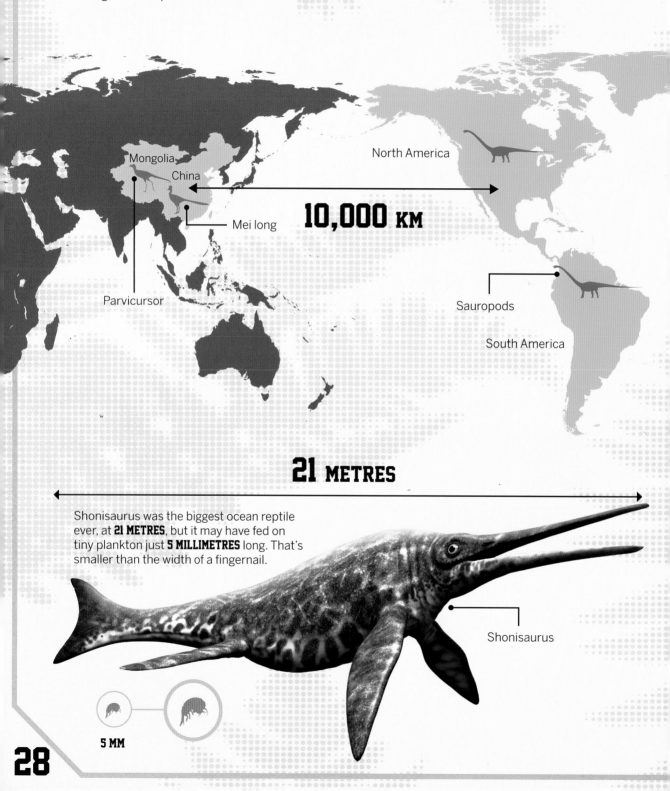

Mongolia
China
Mei long
Parvicursor
North America
10,000 KM
Sauropods
South America

21 METRES

Shonisaurus was the biggest ocean reptile ever, at **21 METRES**, but it may have fed on tiny plankton just **5 MILLIMETRES** long. That's smaller than the width of a fingernail.

Shonisaurus

5 MM

The fossils of Archaeopteryx were the first bird dinosaur fossils found. Archaeopteryx fossils are said to be worth **£10 MILLION**.

Archaeopteryx fossil

Mei long was only **45 CENTIMETRES**, plus a long tail. It slept curled up and could have been small enough to fit in the palm of a hand.

Fully grown, Archaeopteryx was only **50 CENTIMETRES** long. That's shorter than the height of a **10**-year-old's knee.

Archaeopteryx

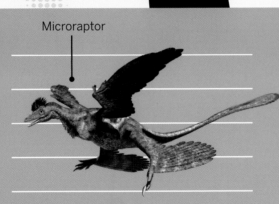

Microraptor

50 CM
40 CM
30 CM
20 CM
10 CM

3 GOOD THINGS ABOUT BEING TINY
1. Can hide from predators
2. Able to eat plentiful food, such as seeds and bugs
3. Only need a small living space

3 BAD THINGS FOR MINI MENACES
1. Tough to travel long distances
2. Lizards and spiders can be scary
3. Weather and larger dinos can destroy habitat

Protoceratops

Protoceratops weighed as much as **2** large humans, but it was tiny compared to its relative, Triceratops, which was **30** times heavier.

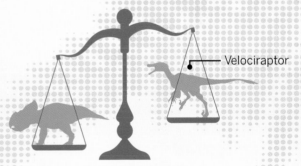

Velociraptor

Protoceratops battled another vicious mini dinosaur, Velociraptor, which weighed just **15 PER CENT** of a Protoceratops.

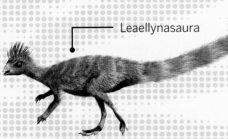

Leaellynasaura

Leaellynasaura had a body, head and neck length of just **50 CENTIMETRES**, with a very long tail it wrapped around itself. It lived in chilly Australian forests, where it was dark for **3** months of the year.

SPEED MACHINES

Take a close-up look at these lightning-quick facts and numbers. Look carefully, though – blink and you'll miss them!

Coelophysis was slim, streamlined and built for speed. Its **3**-clawed feet helped it reach speeds of nearly **50 KM/H**. That's faster than an Olympic sprinter.

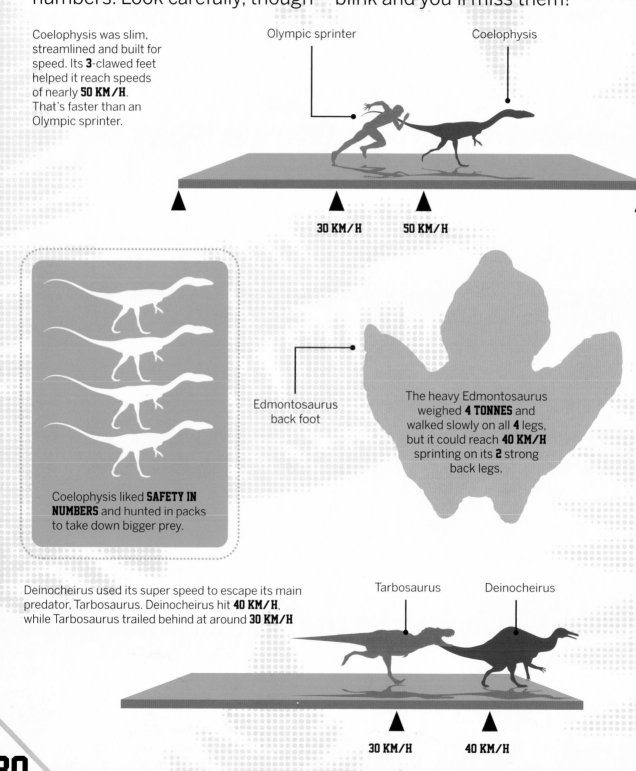

Olympic sprinter

Coelophysis

30 KM/H   50 KM/H

Edmontosaurus back foot

Coelophysis liked **SAFETY IN NUMBERS** and hunted in packs to take down bigger prey.

The heavy Edmontosaurus weighed **4 TONNES** and walked slowly on all **4** legs, but it could reach **40 KM/H** sprinting on its **2** strong back legs.

Deinocheirus used its super speed to escape its main predator, Tarbosaurus. Deinocheirus hit **40 KM/H**, while Tarbosaurus trailed behind at around **30 KM/H**

Tarbosaurus   Deinocheirus

30 KM/H   40 KM/H

60
OSTRICH

Gallimimus looked like an ostrich, and ran like one, too. It was fast, but an ostrich would be about **12 KM/H** faster in a race.

Argentinosaurus is one of the biggest dinosaurs at **80 TONNES**, but it wouldn't win any prizes for sprinting, with a top speed of just **8 KM/H**!

48
GALLIMIMUS

LOSER

Argentinosaurus

Gallimimus

5 SERIOUSLY SPEEDY DINOS

1. Struthiomimus	**UP TO 80 KM/H**
2. Deinonychus	**56 KM/H**
3. Herrerasaurus	**48 KM/H**
4. Gallimimus	**48 KM/H**
5. Megalosaurus	**48 KM/H**

The feathers on Microraptor assisted with gliding and steering, but made the dino a clumsy runner. It could reach **40 KM/H** in the air, but just **20 KM/H** on land.

Microraptor

Ophthalmosaurus

The **4-METRE**-long Ophthalmosaurus was perhaps the fastest marine reptile of the dinosaur age. Its powerful tail helped it blast through the water like a speedy submarine, at **30 KM/H**.

Most marine species struggled to reach **8 KM/H**, which is nearly **3** times slower than Ophthalmosaurus.

ON YOUR MARKS...

Get your running shoes on – you'll need them to keep up with two of the fastest creatures of the dinosaur age!

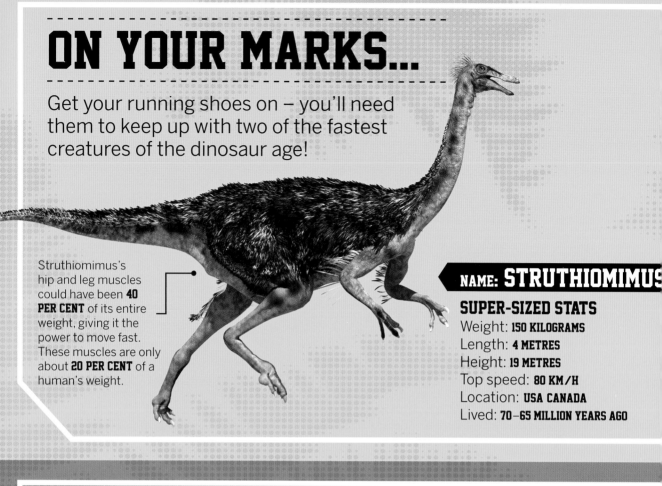

Struthiomimus's hip and leg muscles could have been **40 PER CENT** of its entire weight, giving it the power to move fast. These muscles are only about **20 PER CENT** of a human's weight.

NAME: STRUTHIOMIMUS

SUPER-SIZED STATS
Weight: **150 KILOGRAMS**
Length: **4 METRES**
Height: **19 METRES**
Top speed: **80 KM/H**
Location: **USA CANADA**
Lived: **70–65 MILLION YEARS AGO**

NAME: DEINONYCHUS

SUPER-SIZED STATS
Weight: **60 KILOGRAMS**
Length: **3 METRES**
Top speed: **56 KM/H**
Location: **USA**
Lived: **115–108 MILLION YEARS AGO**

Large wolf

Deinonychus was similar in weight to a large wolf and could kill small dinosaurs on its own.

Struthiomimus would have been nearly twice as fast as champion sprinter Usain Bolt, who can reach speeds of **44 KM/H**.

Usain Bolt

Struthiomimus's speed would be illegal on the island of Guernsey, near France. The speed limit on the roads there is just **56 KM/H**.

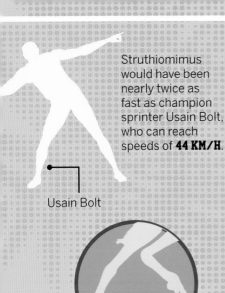

9 M

At top speed, Struthiomimus had a stride of **9 METRES**.

4.7 SECONDS

At full speed, Struthiomimus could run from one end of a football pitch to the other in just **4.7 SECONDS**!

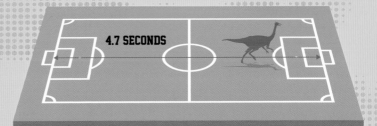

60 KMH

Deinonychus weighed **60 KILOGRAMS**, had **60** razor-sharp teeth for tearing meat and could reach speeds of nearly **60 KM/H**. That's about the speed a small moped motorbike can reach.

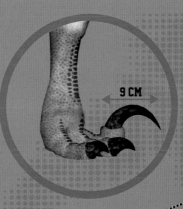

9 CM

The **9-CENTIMETRE** claw on each foot was useful for attacking larger prey, like Tenontosaurus.

3.5 METRES

It's thought that Deinonychus could jump **3.5 METRES**, which is about the height of **2** UK post boxes, to attack prey at speed.

Deinonychus

NUMBER CRUNCH
Deinonychus could have had a walking speed of **10.1 KM/H** and a top running speed **5** times faster. Humans walk at about **4 KM/H**.

WINGED WONDERS

Fascinating dinosaurs and prehistoric reptiles took to the skies, such as the Quetzalcoatlus, Pteranodon and Nyctosaurus. You'll discover lots of high-flying facts on these pages...

Quetzalcoatlus was the largest flying reptile, ever. Its mighty wingspan was **11 METRES**, which is about the size of a Spitfire battle plane.

Spitfire

Quetzalcoatlus

These huge wings helped Quetzalcoatlus reach flying speeds of **36 KM/H**. Some experts think it may have reached speeds of more than **100 KM/H**!

11 METRES

Pterosaurs

On the ground, Quetzalcoatlus stood taller than a giraffe, at nearly **7 METRES**.

5 METRES

Pterosaurs were a family of flying reptiles that filled the skies for over **150 MILLION** years. They had **ZERO** feathers on their wings, which were stretches of skin between their legs and body with a large fourth finger on the outer edges.

The smallest pterosaur was Nemicolopterus. Its wingspan was only **25 CENTIMETRES**, which meant each wing was a bit longer than the length of a pencil.

18 CENTIMETRES

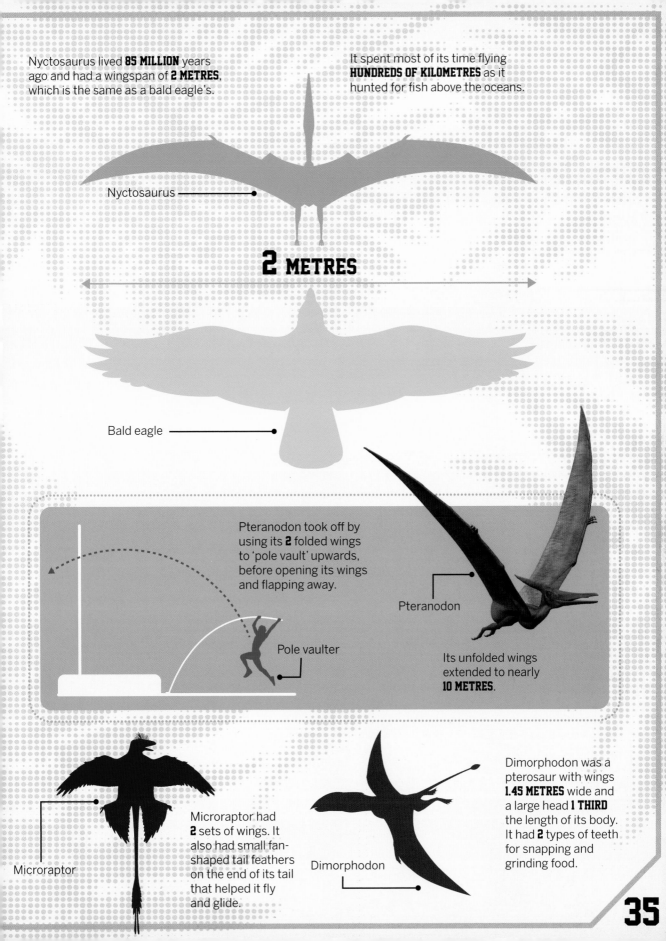

Nyctosaurus lived **85 MILLION** years ago and had a wingspan of **2 METRES**, which is the same as a bald eagle's.

It spent most of its time flying **HUNDREDS OF KILOMETRES** as it hunted for fish above the oceans.

Nyctosaurus

2 METRES

Bald eagle

Pteranodon took off by using its **2** folded wings to 'pole vault' upwards, before opening its wings and flapping away.

Pole vaulter

Pteranodon

Its unfolded wings extended to nearly **10 METRES**.

Microraptor had **2** sets of wings. It also had small fan-shaped tail feathers on the end of its tail that helped it fly and glide.

Microraptor

Dimorphodon

Dimorphodon was a pterosaur with wings **1.45 METRES** wide and a large head **1 THIRD** the length of its body. It had **2** types of teeth for snapping and grinding food.

ROUGH AND TOUGH

Take cover – you're about to see a stash of stats all about the strongest and best-protected creatures ever to roam planet Earth!

Tank

Ankylosaurus

TOP 5 ARMOURED DINOS

Ankylosaurs are often called dinosaur 'tanks' because they had heavily-protected bodies and moved surprisingly fast. Here are the top **5** armoured dinos...

1. ANKYLOSAURUS
2. EUOPLOCEPHALUS
3. SAICHANIA
4. TARCHIA
5. GASTONIA

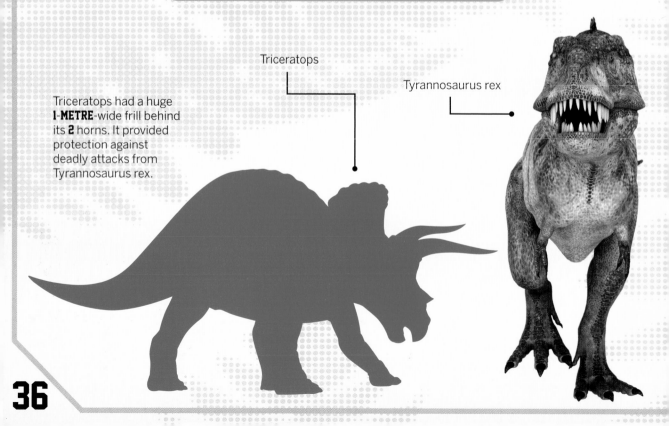

Triceratops had a huge **1-METRE**-wide frill behind its **2** horns. It provided protection against deadly attacks from Tyrannosaurus rex.

Triceratops

Tyrannosaurus rex

Pentaceratops's name means '**5**-horned face', but it actually only had **3** horns. This big beast weighed as much as **3** cars.

Pentaceratops

③
②
①

Hylaeosaurus

Scutellosaurus

50 CM

Scutellosaurus was only about **50 CENTIMETRES** tall, which is the height of an adult's knee. It was covered in hundreds of bony studs to protect it from predators.

The horned Euoplocephalus was **6 METRES** long and weighed as much as **2** polar bears. It had a wide body and was low to the ground, making it difficult for attackers to flip it over in battle.

If attacked by a large predator, the **1-TONNE** Hylaeosaurus may have tucked its legs under its body and crouched down. It was covered in over **100** sharp spikes and bony armour to stop enemies landing a killer bite.

7x2

The **5-METRE** long Kentrosaurus had **7** pairs of tough plates along its neck and back.

Polar bears

Euoplocephalus

NUMBER CRUNCH
More than **900** Kentrosaurus bones were found in one place in Tanzania, Africa.

Scelidosaurus lived about **196 MILLION** years ago and was covered from head to toe in bony studs and spikes. Its armour was coated in keratin, a strong fibre also found in human fingernails.

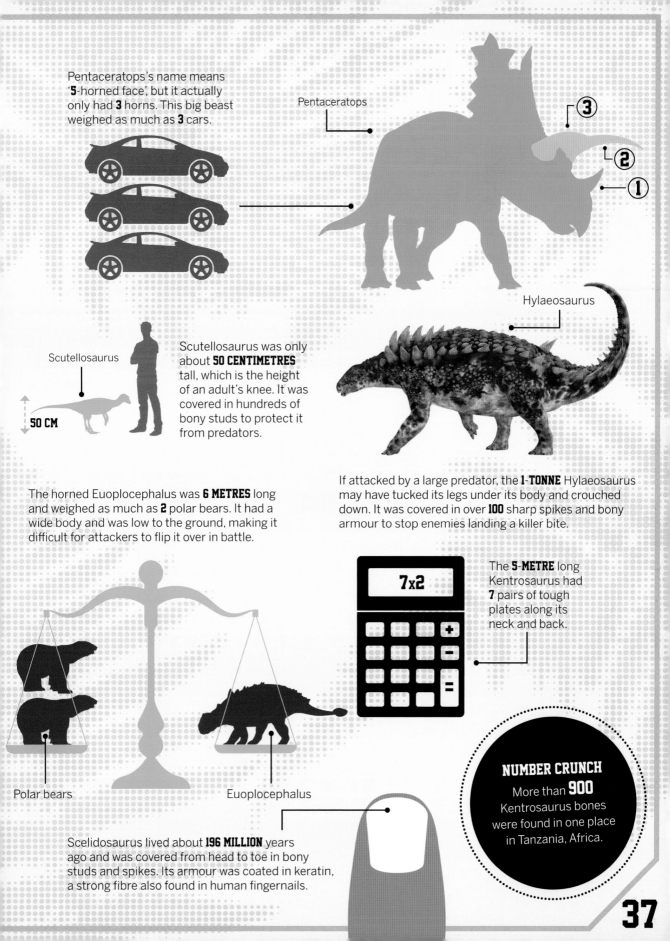

READY TO ATTACK

Coahuilaceratops and Ankylosaurus may have been plant eaters, but they had awesome armour and weapons to fend off attacks from mighty meat eaters. These big beasts were always ready to attack!

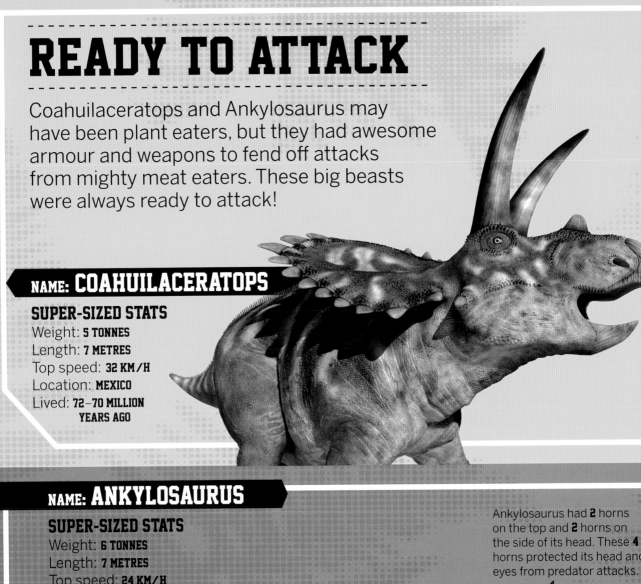

NAME: COAHUILACERATOPS

SUPER-SIZED STATS
Weight: **5 TONNES**
Length: **7 METRES**
Top speed: **32 KM/H**
Location: **MEXICO**
Lived: **72–70 MILLION YEARS AGO**

NAME: ANKYLOSAURUS

SUPER-SIZED STATS
Weight: **6 TONNES**
Length: **7 METRES**
Top speed: **24 KM/H**
Location: **USA**
Lived: **70–65 MILLION YEAERS AGO**

Ankylosaurus had **2** horns on the top and **2** horns on the side of its head. These **4** horns protected its head and eyes from predator attacks.

This heavily-armoured creature's secret weapon was its terrifying tail. It was a heavy club made of **2** bony plates fused together, which it swiped at attackers.

Coahuilaceratops had **2** fierce **1-METRE**-long horns that were the size of broom handles and even longer than the famous spikes of a triceratops.

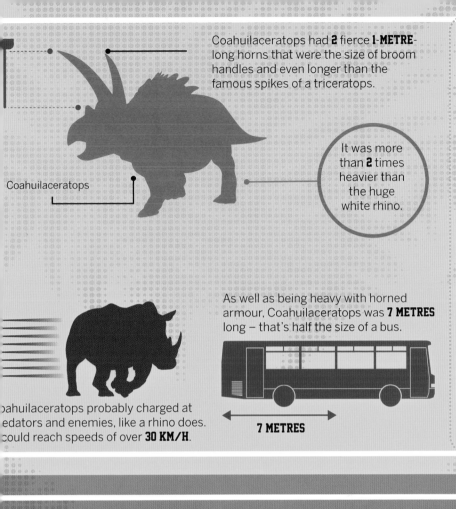

Coahuilaceratops

It was more than **2** times heavier than the huge white rhino.

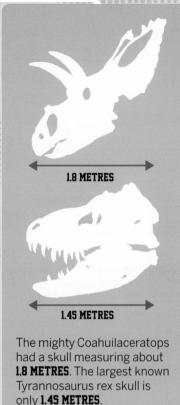

1.8 METRES

1.45 METRES

The mighty Coahuilaceratops had a skull measuring about **1.8 METRES**. The largest known Tyrannosaurus rex skull is only **1.45 METRES**.

As well as being heavy with horned armour, Coahuilaceratops was **7 METRES** long – that's half the size of a bus.

7 METRES

oahuilaceratops probably charged at edators and enemies, like a rhino does. could reach speeds of over **30 KM/H**.

Ankylosaurus had **HUNDREDS** of rounded armour plates over its body. Experts say this was as strong as Kevlar, a fibre used to make bulletproof vests.

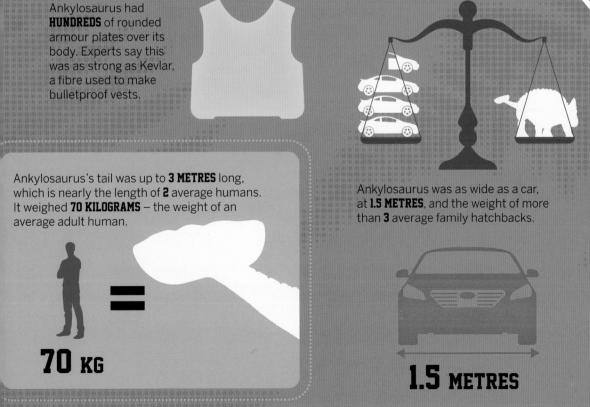

Ankylosaurus's tail was up to **3 METRES** long, which is nearly the length of **2** average humans. It weighed **70 KILOGRAMS** – the weight of an average adult human.

70 KG =

Ankylosaurus was as wide as a car, at **1.5 METRES**, and the weight of more than **3** average family hatchbacks.

1.5 METRES

TELLING A TAIL

These exciting dinos have something very interesting going on behind them – right behind them, actually – in their tails!

CRACK!

Diplodocus

Some scientists think that the **30-TONNE** Diplodocus may have used its **14-METRE**-long tail to make a loud cracking noise to scare other dinosaurs.

To make a cracking sound, Diplodocus's tail would have needed to move at more than **1,206 KM/H**. That's nearly as fast as a jet plane has to travel to break the sound barrier.

The longest tail ever belonged to the sauropod Amphicoelias. It was about **30 METRES**, which is **4** times longer than **1** rugby goalpost.

Rugby goalpost

x4

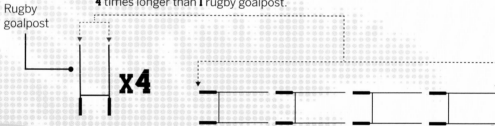

Amphicoelias

30 CM

16 CM

Psittacosaurus had a **30-CENTIMETRE**-long tail. It was covered in about **100** brightly-coloured quills (feathers), which were each up to **16 CENTIMETRES**.

Psittacosaurus

30 CM

Ankylosaurus

Ankylosaurus's deadly club tail was **30 CENTIMETRES** thick. That's wider than a letterbox on a door.

Ankylosaur's tail

Sugar

Edmontonia

The tail of Euoplocephalus, which was an Ankylosaur, was **2.5 METRES** long and weighed as much as **30** bags of sugar.

Edmontonia had small spikes on its tail. Despite being half the height and weight of a Tyrannosaurus rex, at about **3 METRES** and **3 TONNES**, its sharp tail was a vicious weapon against predators.

Coelophysis may have had a tail about **40 PER CENT** the length of its whole body, at over **1 METRE**. Its long tail helped it balance and to reach speeds of nearly **50 KM/H**.

Coelophysis

Tyrannosaurus rex's tail was between **3** and **4 METRES** long, but it wasn't very bendy. It was held straight out to balance the forward lean of its upper body.

When the **6-METRE**-long Megalosaurus was first discovered in **1824**, scientists thought that dinosaurs dragged their long tails along the ground, like lizards. They now know most dinos held their tails high.

Tyrannosaurus rex

3-4 METRES

T. rex comes from a group called tetanurans, which means 'still tails'.

'EYE' DON'T BELIEVE IT!

You'll need to keep a close eye on this stack of super stats and numbers all about dinosaur vision and sight. It's a great spectacle!

Stenonychosaurus

The bird-like predator Stenonychosaurus had eyes **4.5 CENTIMETRES** wide, which is nearly **2** times the size of a human eye.

Human eye

Stenonychosaurus eye

4.5 CENTIMETRES

Stenonychosaurus had **3** eyelids – an upper and a lower – like humans do, plus a third protective eyelid called the nictitating membrane.

NUMBER CRUNCH
The eye sockets of the largest Tyrannosaurus rex ever found were **10.5 CENTIMETRES** in width, which meant it had eyeballs bigger than tennis balls!

Stenonychosaurus had binocular eyesight, which means the field of vision in its **2** eyes crossed over in front of its beak, creating a **3D** picture that helped it judge distances well.

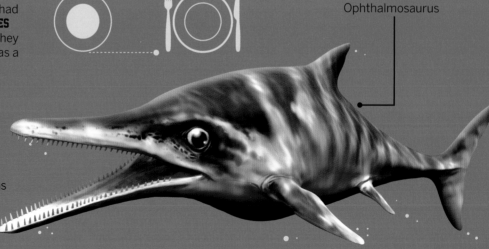

The sea reptile Ophthalmosaurus had eyes **23 CENTIMETRES** wide. That means they were nearly as big as a dinner plate!

Ophthalmosaurus

Its huge eyes helped it to see prey when it dived more than **100 METRES** into the depths of the ocean.

The **2-TONNE** Euoplocephalus was so well protected, it even had armoured eyelids to protect its eyes!

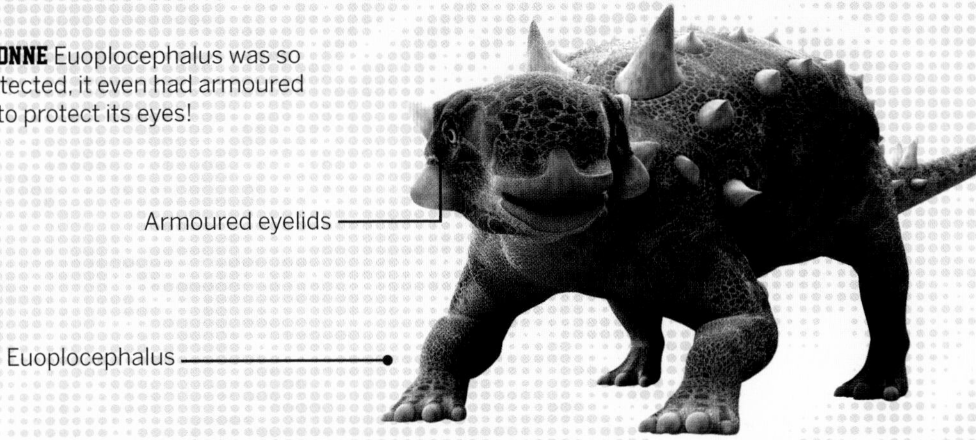

Armoured eyelids

Euoplocephalus

Plant eaters like Nigersaurus had eyes on the sides of their head. This gave them a **350-DEGREE** view of their surroundings.

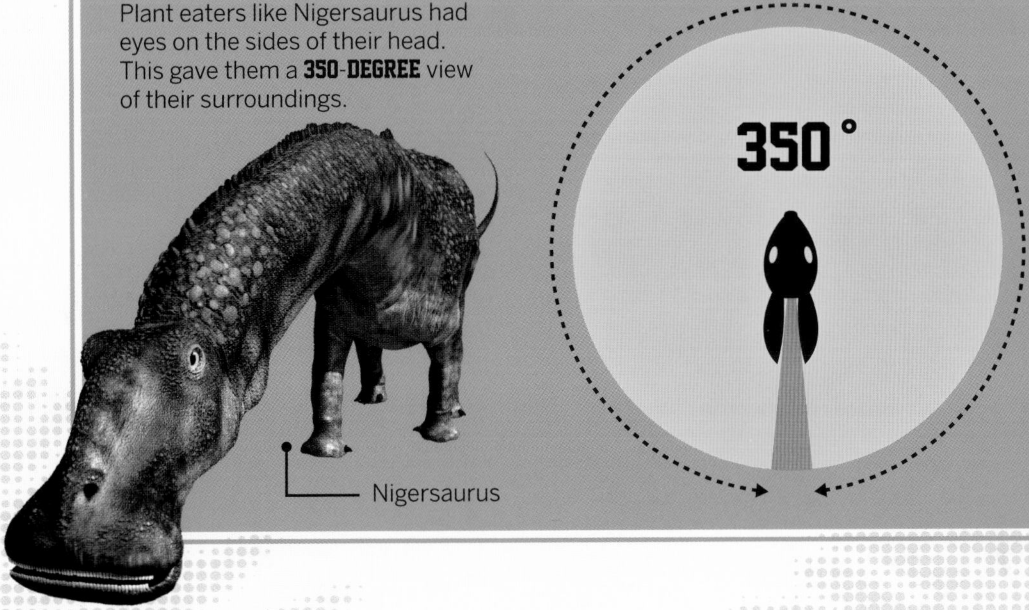

350°

Nigersaurus

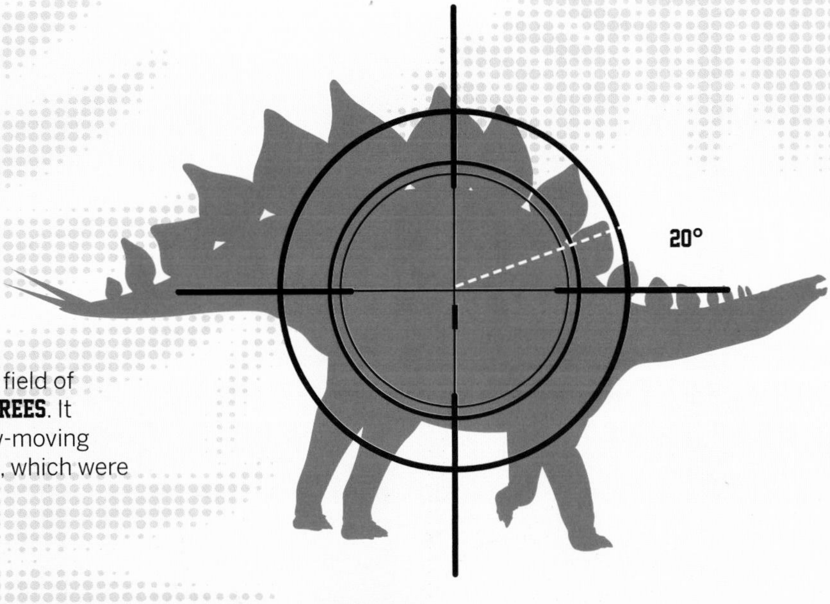

Allosaurus only had a field of vision of about **20 DEGREES**. It hunted large and slow-moving prey like Stegosaurus, which were easy for it to spot.

20°

BITE-SIZED FACTS

Here's plenty of exciting info to chew over! It's all about the teeth, jaws and mouths of some mighty dinosaurs.

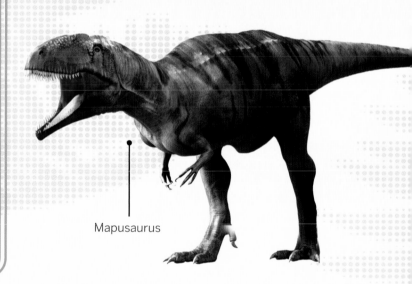

Citipati

The **3-METRE**-long Citipati was a meat-eating feathered dinosaur. It didn't have proper teeth – instead it had **2** bony prongs on the roof of its mouth to rip prey apart.

The **6-TONNE** killer Mapusaurus had smooth, curved teeth with a knife-like edge for slicing flesh rather than crushing bones. Experts think it may have wounded much larger prey with its teeth and then waited minutes, hours or even days for the victim to finally die before it ate it.

Mapusaurus tooth

Mapusaurus

Shunosaurus

Shunosaurus was **12 METRES** long and it had about **26** teeth in each half of its lower jaw. That's more than any other sauropod.

The Pteranodon's frightening jaws were **1.2 METRES** long, which is twice the length of an adult's arm.

Pteranodon

It had a wingspan of **10 METRES**, had **ZERO** teeth and swallowed small fish and mammals whole.

10 METRES

Bristles

Nigersaurus had around **500 TEETH** in total. Its jaw was lined with **2** rows of about **60** teeth, behind which were rows of replacement teeth.

The lower jaw of flying reptile Pterodaustro was filled with about **500** bristles, each **4 CENTIMETRES** long. They sieved and sorted tiny creatures in shallow rivers and lakes.

Tyrannosaurus rex had **50** teeth, each shaped like a bullet with a very sharp edge.

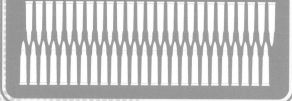

Protoceratops

A Diplodocus's head was just **60 CENTIMETRES** long and its mouth was filled with lots of peg-like teeth. These were great for uprooting plants and taking leaves off trees.

Protoceratops had **2** pairs of sharp teeth at the front of its mouth, but its parrot-like beak inflicted more damage to attackers.

MIGHTY MOUTHS

Luckily for Edmontosaurus, it lived in a different land to the jaw-dropping predator Tarbosaurus. Both these heavyweight dinos were tooth-tastic creatures with mighty mouths.

NAME: **TARBOSAURUS**

SUPER-SIZED STATS
Weight: **5 TONNES**
Length: **10 METRES**
Top speed: **30 KM/H**
Location: **ASIA**
Lived: **70–65 MILLION YEARS AGO**

NAME: **EDMONTOSAURUS**

SUPER-SIZED STATS
Weight: **4 TONNES**
Length: **9 METRES**
Top speed: **40 KM/H**
Location: **USA, CANADA**
Lived: **70–65 MILLION YEARS AGO**

1ST

Thanks to its mighty jaws and bone-crushing teeth, Tarbosaurus was the **NO. 1** predator **70 MILLION YEARS** ago in China and Mongolia.

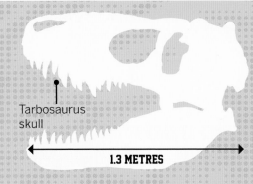

Tarbosaurus skull

1.3 METRES

Tarbosaurus had a skull size of **1.3 METRES**, which is **4** times bigger than that of a modern wolf's skull.

Wolf

Tarbosaurus means 'alarming lizard'. With razor-sharp teeth **10-20 CENTIMETRES** long, it would have alarmed predators like Barsboldia.

It's said to have had the second strongest bite of all the predator dinosaurs, behind Tyrannosaurus rex, and **5** times more powerful than a lion.

Tarbosaurus

Lion

---

x1,000

Edmontosaurus takes the crown for the dinosaur with the most teeth. It had more than **1000** diamond-shaped teeth, all lined up in blocks called 'dental batteries'.

Edmontosaurus roamed North America in herds of **50** or more for protection against other dinosaurs.

Edmontosaurus

METRE

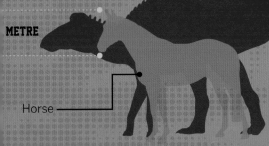

Much like a horse, Edmontosaurus had a head over **1 METRE** long, which was broad and strong.

Horse

NUMBER CRUNCH
Edmontosaurus probably munched more than **100 KG** of vegetation each day, which is about the weight of **5** mountain bikes.

DINNER TIME

Don't get in the way of this bunch when they're hungry! Colossal plant eaters, meat-eating killers and picky termite munchers all fancy a bite to eat right now...

Meat-eating carnivores, like Spinosaurus, got lots of energy from their food. They probably didn't need to eat for **3** or **4 DAYS** after a big meal.

MONDAY	TUESDAY	WEDNESDAY	THURSDAY	FRIDAY	SATURDAY	SUNDAY
🍽					🍽	

20 HOURS

Large sauropods, which weighed up to **100 TONNES**, probably had to eat for about **20 HOURS** each day to get enough energy for their massive bodies.

Tyrannosaurus rex

At **12 METRES** long, Tyrannosaurus rex was as big as a bus. It had tiny **1-METRE**-long arms, however, that couldn't reach up to its mouth to put food into it.

Pelecanimimus

The Pelecanimimus had **220** teeth, the most of any dinosaur predator. It stored food in a skin sac in its throat.

Brachiosaurus

Brachiosaurus could scoff around **400 KILOGRAMS** of plants in a single day, which is the weight of **8** large dogs.

400 KG

The **30-METRE**-long Barosaurus may have used stomach bacteria to help digest the huge amount of plants it ate, which is how a cow digests food.

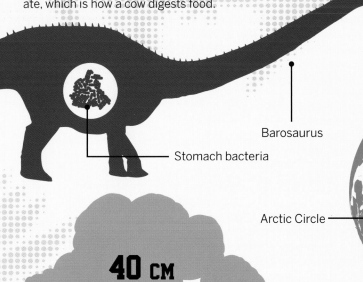

Stomach bacteria

Barosaurus

Stenonychosaurus

Arctic Circle

40 CM

Stenonychosaurus may have lived for **5** continuous months or more in the freezing Arctic Circle. It would have eaten anything it could find to survive.

Fossilized coprolites (poo) that have been uncovered have been around **40 CENTIMETRES** wide. Experts think they probably came from a sauropod and show that it ate plants, seeds and leaves.

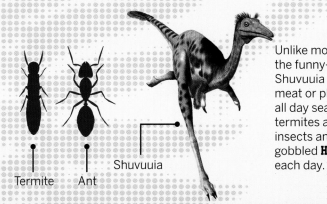

Unlike most dinosaurs, the funny-looking Shuvuuia didn't eat meat or plants. It spent all day searching for termites and other insects and would have gobbled **HUNDREDS** each day.

Termite Ant

Shuvuuia

NUMBER CRUNCH
A coprolite found in **1995** in Canada was **42 CENTIMETRES** long. It contained different dinosaur bones and may have been from a hungry T. rex.

A BITE TO EAT

These two curious creatures have completely different dinnertime routines and diets, but they're both fascinating to study as they search for food!

The killer Carcharodontosaurus was nearly as big as a T. rex. It had over **60** saw-like teeth, each up to **20 CENTIMETRES** long for ripping and slashing meat.

NAME: **CARCHARODONTOSAURUS**

SUPER-SIZED STATS
Weight: **7 TONNES**
Length: **13 METRES**
Top speed: **30 KM/H**
Location: **AFRICA**
Lived: **105–94 MILLION YEARS AGO**

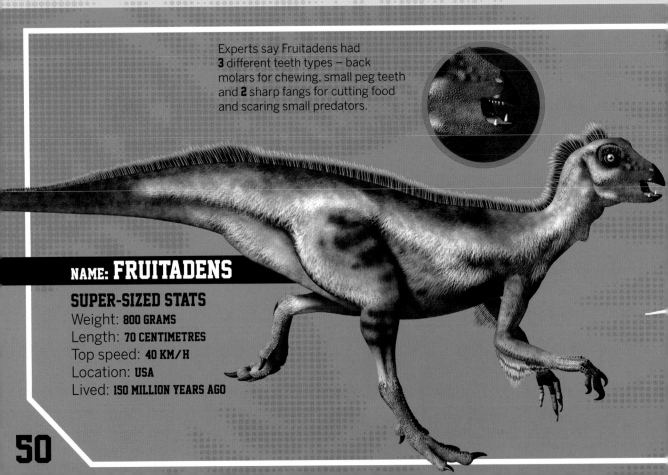

Experts say Fruitadens had **3** different teeth types – back molars for chewing, small peg teeth and **2** sharp fangs for cutting food and scaring small predators.

NAME: **FRUITADENS**

SUPER-SIZED STATS
Weight: **800 GRAMS**
Length: **70 CENTIMETRES**
Top speed: **40 KM/H**
Location: **USA**
Lived: **150 MILLION YEARS AGO**

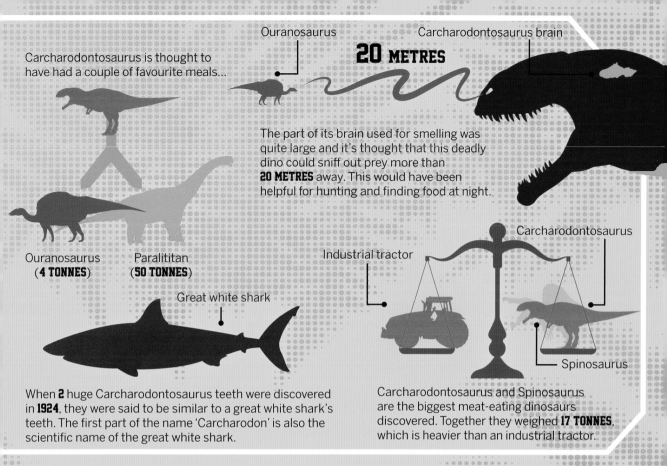

Carcharodontosaurus is thought to have had a couple of favourite meals...

Ouranosaurus

20 METRES

Carcharodontosaurus brain

The part of its brain used for smelling was quite large and it's thought that this deadly dino could sniff out prey more than **20 METRES** away. This would have been helpful for hunting and finding food at night.

Ouranosaurus (**4 TONNES**)

Paralititan (**50 TONNES**)

Great white shark

Industrial tractor

Carcharodontosaurus

Spinosaurus

When **2** huge Carcharodontosaurus teeth were discovered in **1924**, they were said to be similar to a great white shark's teeth. The first part of the name 'Carcharodon' is also the scientific name of the great white shark.

Carcharodontosaurus and Spinosaurus are the biggest meat-eating dinosaurs discovered. Together they weighed **17 TONNES**, which is heavier than an industrial tractor.

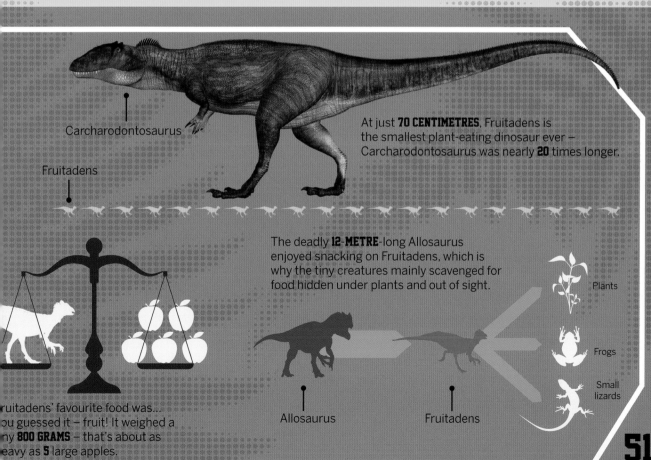

Carcharodontosaurus

Fruitadens

At just **70 CENTIMETRES**, Fruitadens is the smallest plant-eating dinosaur ever – Carcharodontosaurus was nearly **20** times longer.

The deadly **12-METRE**-long Allosaurus enjoyed snacking on Fruitadens, which is why the tiny creatures mainly scavenged for food hidden under plants and out of sight.

Plants

Frogs

Small lizards

Allosaurus

Fruitadens

ruitadens' favourite food was... ou guessed it – fruit! It weighed a ny **800 GRAMS** – that's about as eavy as **5** large apples.

UNDER THE SEA

While dinosaurs ruled the land, incredible sea reptiles lived in the nearby waters. Let's dive deep to discover some dazzling details...

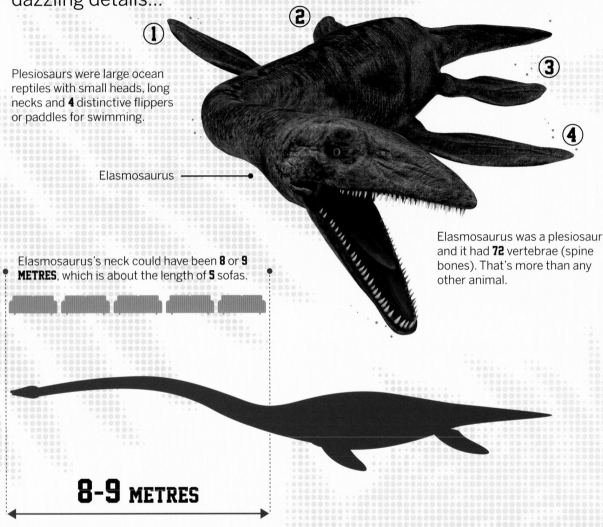

① ② ③ ④

Plesiosaurs were large ocean reptiles with small heads, long necks and **4** distinctive flippers or paddles for swimming.

Elasmosaurus

Elasmosaurus was a plesiosaur and it had **72** vertebrae (spine bones). That's more than any other animal.

Elasmosaurus's neck could have been **8** or **9 METRES**, which is about the length of **5** sofas.

8-9 METRES

Ophthalmosaurus was a big ocean hunter. It weighed **1 TONNE** and was about **4 METRES** long. Its long jaws were adapted for clamping on to squid and fish and it breathed air at least once every **20 MINUTES**.

Ophthalmosaurus

4 METRES

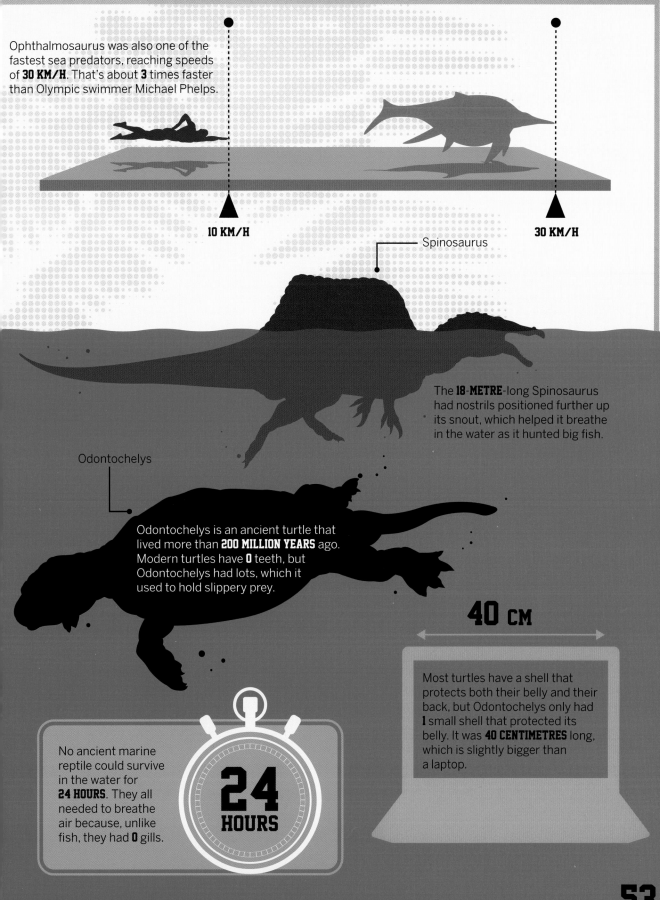

Ophthalmosaurus was also one of the fastest sea predators, reaching speeds of **30 KM/H**. That's about **3** times faster than Olympic swimmer Michael Phelps.

10 KM/H

30 KM/H

Spinosaurus

The **18-METRE**-long Spinosaurus had nostrils positioned further up its snout, which helped it breathe in the water as it hunted big fish.

Odontochelys

Odontochelys is an ancient turtle that lived more than **200 MILLION YEARS** ago. Modern turtles have **0** teeth, but Odontochelys had lots, which it used to hold slippery prey.

40 CM

Most turtles have a shell that protects both their belly and their back, but Odontochelys only had **1** small shell that protected its belly. It was **40 CENTIMETRES** long, which is slightly bigger than a laptop.

No ancient marine reptile could survive in the water for **24 HOURS**. They all needed to breathe air because, unlike fish, they had **0** gills.

24 HOURS

SUPER SEA BATTLE

It's battle of the massive sea reptiles! These water-based ancient wonders would have been an incredible sight in the oceans of North America and Europe.

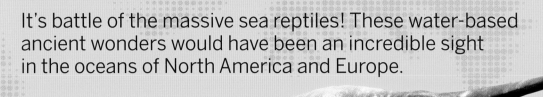

NAME: SHONISAURUS

SUPER-SIZED STATS
Weight: **20 TONNES**
Length: **21 METRES**
Top speed: **15 KM/H**
Location: **USA CANADA**
Lived: **216–203 MILLION YEARS AGO**

NAME: LIOPLEURODON

SUPER-SIZED STATS
Weight: **6 TONNES**
Length: **15 METRES**
Top speed: **7 KM/H**
Location: **NORTHERN EUROPE**
Lived: **165–145 MILLION YEARS AGO**

Liopleurodon may have had up to **100** sharp teeth. Some were longer than an adult's foot!

Shonisaurus takes the title for the biggest sea reptile. It was about **21 METRES** long, and some could grow up to **26 METRES**. That's twice the size of a great white shark.

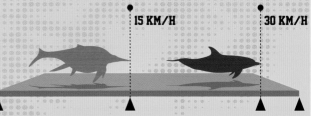

0

That's the number of teeth Shonisaurus had. It used its strong mouth and tongue to suck up squid and fish.

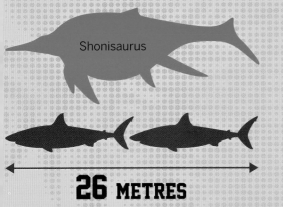

Shonisaurus

26 METRES

Its **4** long, slender fins were **3 METRES**, which is the same as **3** wheelie bins stacked on top of each other.

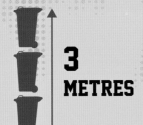

3 METRES

15 KM/H   **30 KM/H**

Shonisaurus was big but probably quite slow. It could only reach a top speed of **15 KM/H**, which is about **50 PER CENT** of a bottlenose dolphin's speed.

Shonisaurus weighed a colossal **20 TONNES**. That's more than **3** times bigger than a T. rex.

x3

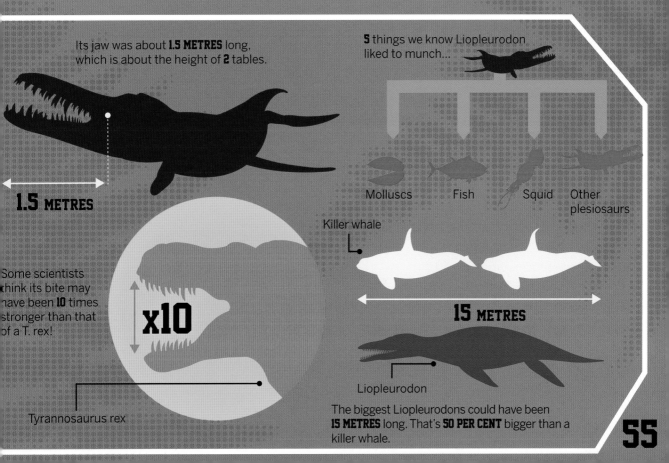

Its jaw was about **1.5 METRES** long, which is about the height of **2** tables.

1.5 METRES

Some scientists think its bite may have been **10** times stronger than that of a T. rex!

x10

Tyrannosaurus rex

5 things we know Liopleurodon liked to munch...

Molluscs   Fish   Squid   Other plesiosaurs

Killer whale

15 METRES

Liopleurodon

The biggest Liopleurodons could have been **15 METRES** long. That's **50 PER CENT** bigger than a killer whale.

MYTHS AND MYSTERIES

If you're puzzled by certain dinosaur myths and mysteries, don't worry! You will get plenty of answers over the next four pages.

If you ever see a Tyrannosaurus rex footprint and think it's small, there's a reason. Its feet were **1 METRE** long, but its footprints are half that size because it walked on its toes.

0.5 METRES

T. rex footprint

2 THINGS T. REX MAY HAVE USED ITS SMALL ARMS FOR...

1. Pushing up from the ground if it fell over

2. Holding struggling prey

Amargasaurus

Why did the early plant-eating dinosaurs from **220 MILLION YEARS** ago not eat grasses or fruits? Back then there weren't any – just plants like ferns and conifer trees.

Remains of stones, called gastroliths, have been found in the fossils of big plant-eating sauropods like the **4-TONNE** Amargasaurus. They may have swallowed stones to provide much needed mineral content to their diet.

The flying Nyctosaurus had a giant head crest, which was **4** times longer than its skull. This may have been covered in skin that worked like a ship's sail when it was gliding.

Nyctosaurus

Iguanodon

When the **3-TONNE** Iguanodon's remains were found in the **1800s**, scientists were confused and thought its thumb was actually a nose horn.

The word 'dinosaur' was first used by an English scientist called Richard Owen in **1842**. The first **3** dinosaur members he classed were Megalosaurus, Hylaeosaurus and Iguanodon.

Megalosaurus

Hylaeosaurus

Iguanodon

Omeisaurus had a giant **8-METRE** neck, which was huge compared to its **8-TONNE** body. How was it able to stand? It had strong muscles and lightweight bones.

Parasaurolophus had a distinctive crest on its head that was up to **1.8 METRES** long. It was probably used to make a noise like a trombone to communicate with dinosaurs in its herd.

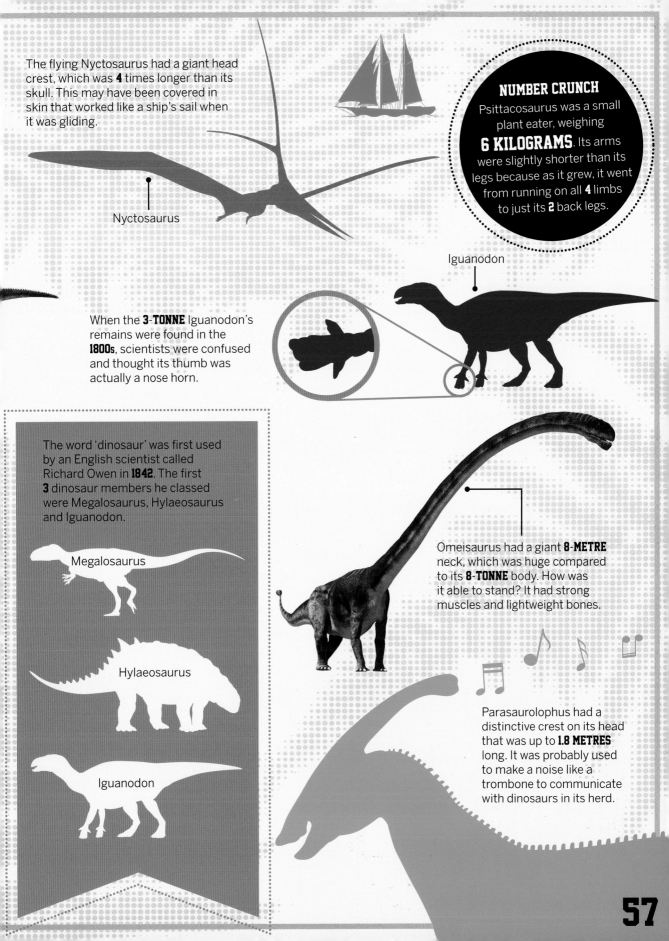

MORE MYTHS AND MYSTERIES

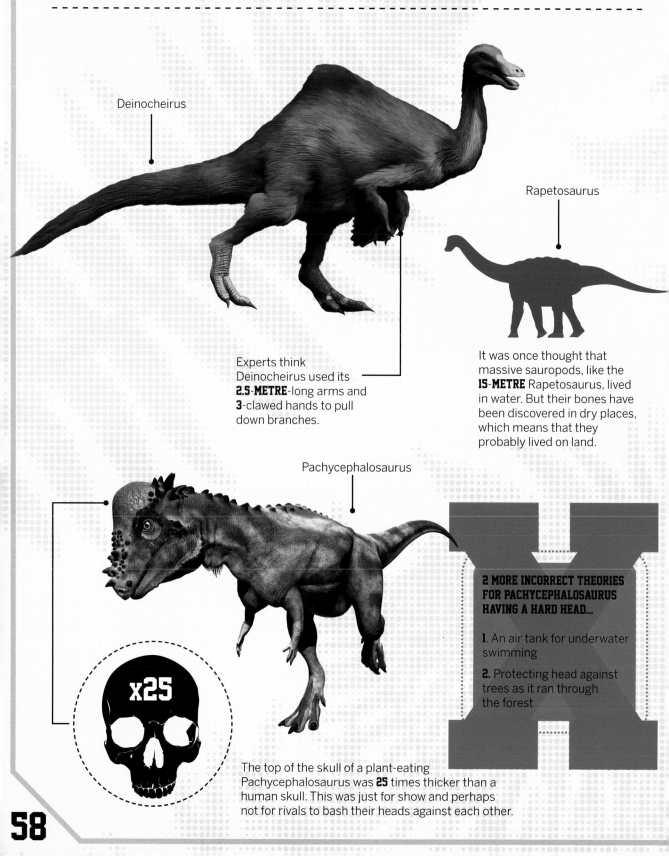

Deinocheirus

Rapetosaurus

Experts think Deinocheirus used its **2.5-METRE**-long arms and **3**-clawed hands to pull down branches.

It was once thought that massive sauropods, like the **15-METRE** Rapetosaurus, lived in water. But their bones have been discovered in dry places, which means that they probably lived on land.

Pachycephalosaurus

x25

2 MORE INCORRECT THEORIES FOR PACHYCEPHALOSAURUS HAVING A HARD HEAD...

1. An air tank for underwater swimming

2. Protecting head against trees as it ran through the forest

The top of the skull of a plant-eating Pachycephalosaurus was **25** times thicker than a human skull. This was just for show and perhaps not for rivals to bash their heads against each other.

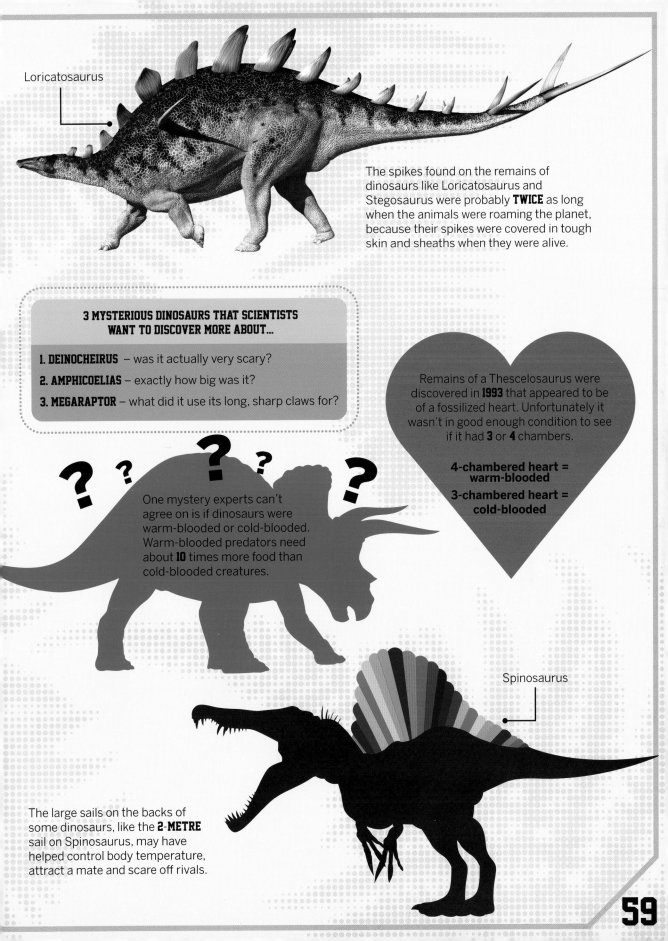

Loricatosaurus

The spikes found on the remains of dinosaurs like Loricatosaurus and Stegosaurus were probably **TWICE** as long when the animals were roaming the planet, because their spikes were covered in tough skin and sheaths when they were alive.

3 MYSTERIOUS DINOSAURS THAT SCIENTISTS WANT TO DISCOVER MORE ABOUT...

1. **DEINOCHEIRUS** – was it actually very scary?
2. **AMPHICOELIAS** – exactly how big was it?
3. **MEGARAPTOR** – what did it use its long, sharp claws for?

Remains of a Thescelosaurus were discovered in **1993** that appeared to be of a fossilized heart. Unfortunately it wasn't in good enough condition to see if it had **3** or **4** chambers.

4-chambered heart = warm-blooded

3-chambered heart = cold-blooded

One mystery experts can't agree on is if dinosaurs were warm-blooded or cold-blooded. Warm-blooded predators need about **10** times more food than cold-blooded creatures.

Spinosaurus

The large sails on the backs of some dinosaurs, like the **2-METRE** sail on Spinosaurus, may have helped control body temperature, attract a mate and scare off rivals.

HEAD MASTERS

You're heading for some thrilling facts now, all about the super and special skulls of these mighty dinosaurs.

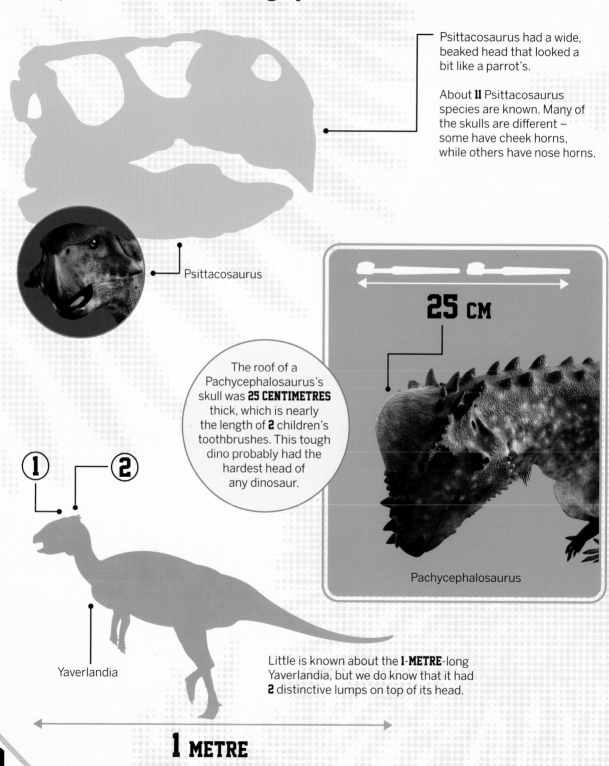

Psittacosaurus had a wide, beaked head that looked a bit like a parrot's.

About **11** Psittacosaurus species are known. Many of the skulls are different – some have cheek horns, while others have nose horns.

Psittacosaurus

25 CM

The roof of a Pachycephalosaurus's skull was **25 CENTIMETRES** thick, which is nearly the length of **2** children's toothbrushes. This tough dino probably had the hardest head of any dinosaur.

① ②

Yaverlandia

Little is known about the **1-METRE**-long Yaverlandia, but we do know that it had **2** distinctive lumps on top of its head.

Pachycephalosaurus

1 METRE

The **2**-legged predator Cryolophosaurus was **6 METRES** long with a crazy curved crest on its head.

Cryolophosaurus

Nigersaurus wins the award for having the weirdest head shape. The widest part of this **2-TONNE** plant eater's head was its massive mouth.

Nigersaurus

Nigersaurus skull

The **5-TONNE** Coahuilaceratops had a **1.8-METRE** skull with a short, stumpy nose horn and a strong, beak-like mouth.

Nigersaurus's skull was covered in lots of holes that made its huge head lighter and easier to raise.

Coahuilaceratops

NUMBER CRUNCH
15 gigantic Tyrannosaurus rex skulls have been discovered around the world with about **90 PER CENT** or more of their structure intact.

The function of the long crest on Pteranodon's skull was probably to attract a mate.

The mighty Pteranodon could fly at speeds of up to **40 KM/H**, thanks to its enormous **10-METRE** wingspan.

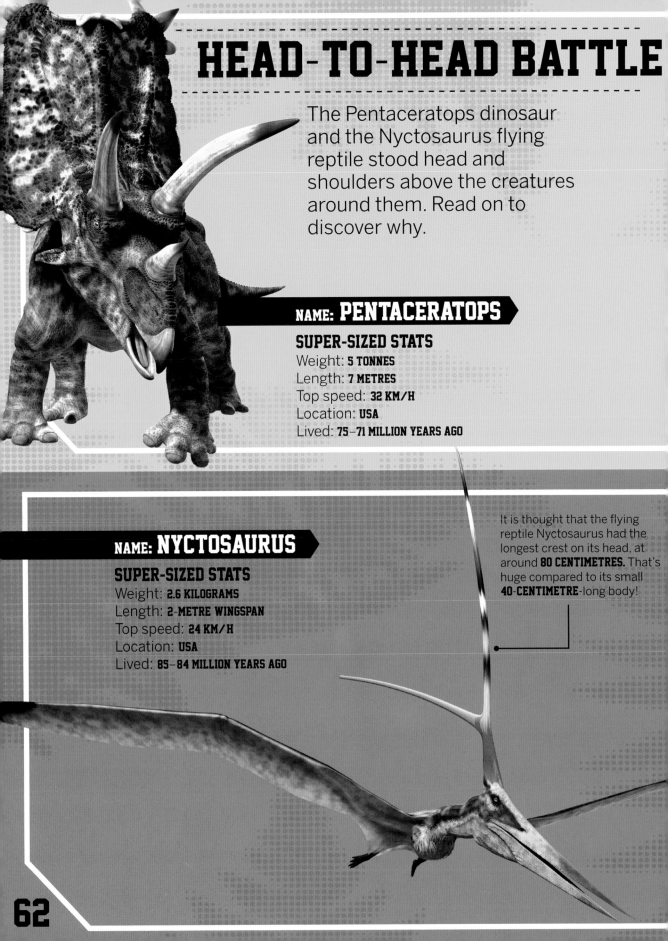

HEAD-TO-HEAD BATTLE

The Pentaceratops dinosaur and the Nyctosaurus flying reptile stood head and shoulders above the creatures around them. Read on to discover why.

NAME: PENTACERATOPS

SUPER-SIZED STATS
Weight: **5 TONNES**
Length: **7 METRES**
Top speed: **32 KM/H**
Location: **USA**
Lived: **75–71 MILLION YEARS AGO**

NAME: NYCTOSAURUS

SUPER-SIZED STATS
Weight: **2.6 KILOGRAMS**
Length: **2-METRE WINGSPAN**
Top speed: **24 KM/H**
Location: **USA**
Lived: **85–84 MILLION YEARS AGO**

It is thought that the flying reptile Nyctosaurus had the longest crest on its head, at around **80 CENTIMETRES.** That's huge compared to its small **40-CENTIMETRE**-long body!

From the tip of its mouth to the top of its head frill, Pentaceratops's head measured up to **3 METRES**. It had the largest head of any land animal, ever.

3 METRES

Walrus tusk

Its head was nearly **5 TIMES** the size of Diplodocus's head.

Pentaceratops horn

Its **2** largest horns were more than **1 METRE** long, which is the same length as the tusks of a male walrus.

The frill at the back of Pentaceratops's head had **2** large holes in it, which were covered with skin. They made the head lighter and easier to move.

4 POSSIBLE REASONS WHY PENTACERATOPS HAD SUCH A BIG HEAD...

1. The large frill worked like a satellite to collect sound.
2. Huge head helped scare off predators, like T. rex.
3. The giant horns could be rammed into attackers.
4. The colourful frill helped attract partners.

Nyctosaurus's head crest was very long, but its wingspan was even longer, at around **2 METRES**. That's bigger than the size of a **40-INCH TV**.

Nyctosaurus

In the **21ST CENTURY**, **2** Nyctosaurus fossils were discovered that had the large Y-shaped crest. Some experts think this belongs to the male of the species, and that females have a shorter crest.

2 METRES

Nyctosaurus had **2** small back legs that weren't very good for running or walking. It was a great flier though, and may have spent more than **20 HOURS** each day flying and searching for food.

20 HOURS

NUMBER CRUNCH
The crest of a Nyctosaurus was **4** times the size of its skull.

SPIKY STUFF

Check out these sharp-suited dinosaur stats. Don't get too close though, because these prickly and pointed creatures could do some serious damage!

Amargasaurus's neck was covered in **9** rows of paired spikes. That's **18** super-sharp spikes to scare off predators.

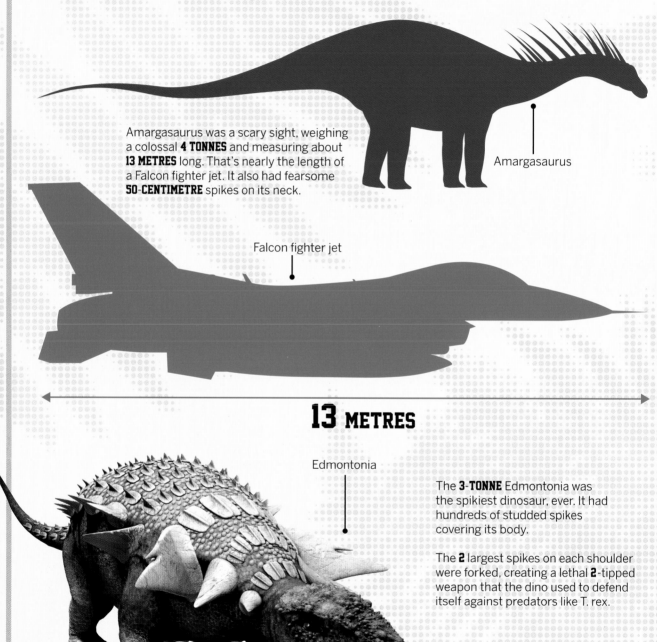

Amargasaurus was a scary sight, weighing a colossal **4 TONNES** and measuring about **13 METRES** long. That's nearly the length of a Falcon fighter jet. It also had fearsome **50-CENTIMETRE** spikes on its neck.

Amargasaurus

Falcon fighter jet

13 METRES

Edmontonia

The **3-TONNE** Edmontonia was the spikiest dinosaur, ever. It had hundreds of studded spikes covering its body.

The **2** largest spikes on each shoulder were forked, creating a lethal **2**-tipped weapon that the dino used to defend itself against predators like T. rex.

With more than **100** teeth for chewing plants, the Iguanodon probably used its spiked thumbs for self-defence and not for collecting food.

Brachiosaurus

Brachiosaurus may have had lots of small spikes, called scutes, along its massive **10-METRE** neck.

Iguanodon

Not all spikes were for defence. The **5-METRE**-long Pachycephalosaurus had spikes on its head that helped attract partners.

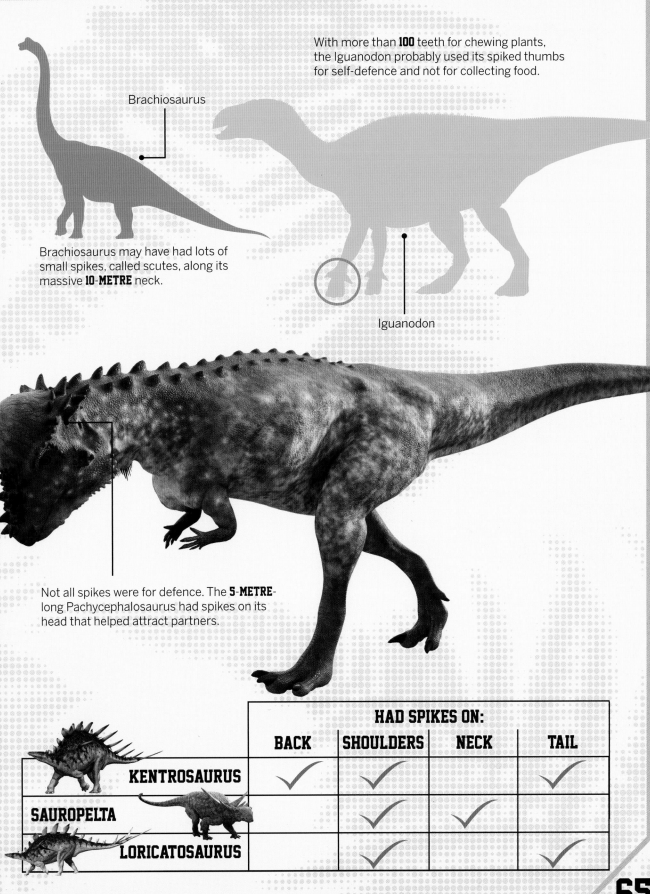

	HAD SPIKES ON:			
	BACK	**SHOULDERS**	**NECK**	**TAIL**
KENTROSAURUS	✓	✓		✓
SAUROPELTA		✓	✓	
LORICATOSAURUS		✓		✓

A POINT TO PROVE

These **TWO** sharp-edged stegosaurs used their giant spikes and plates to really make a point to predators around them.

NAME: **STEGOSAURUS**

SUPER-SIZED STATS
Weight: **3.5 TONNES**
Length: **7 METRES**
Top speed: **16 KM/H**
Location: **USA**
Lived: **155–145 MILLION YEARS AGO**

NAME: **LORICATOSAURUS**

SUPER-SIZED STATS
Weight: **2 TONNES**
Length: **6 METRES**
Top speed: **16 KM/H**
Location: **EUROPE**
Lived: **164–160 MILLION YEARS AGO**

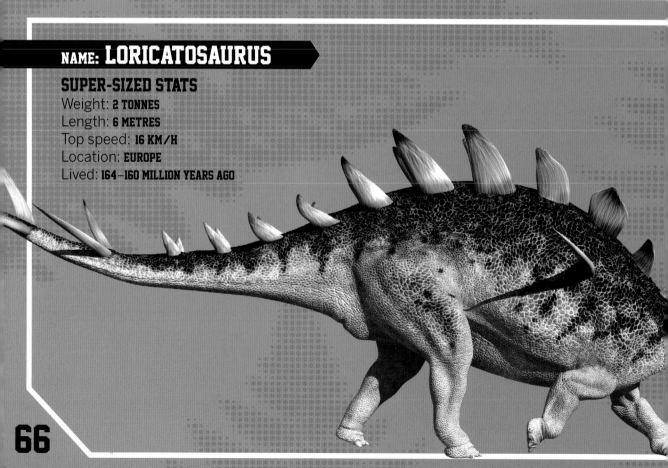

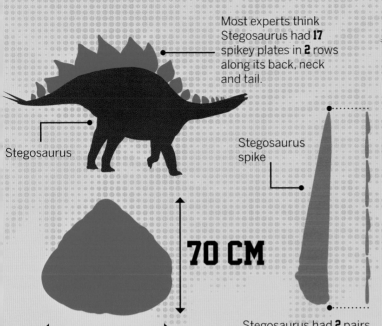

Most experts think Stegosaurus had **17** spikey plates in **2** rows along its back, neck and tail.

Stegosaurus

Stegosaurus spike

Its back legs were nearly double the size of its front legs. This raised its height, made it look frightening and lifted its spikes to nearly **4 METRES** in the air.

70 CM

80 CM

The biggest plates were **70 CENTIMETRES** tall and **80 CENTIMETRES** wide.

Stegosaurus had **2** pairs of sharp spikes on its tail, each about **80 CENTIMETRES** long. These prickles were **4** times bigger than a cutlery knife and were a fierce weapon against attackers.

10,000,000

Stegosaurus survived for around **10 MILLION YEARS**, which is a long time for a dinosaur. That's **2.5** times longer than its earlier spiky relative, Loricatosaurus.

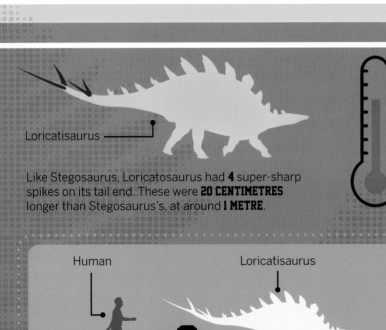

Loricatisaurus

The prickly plates may have controlled Loricatosaurus's body temperature. They could have attracted heat to **INCREASE** warmth, or let heat escape to **DECREASE** temperature.

Like Stegosaurus, Loricatosaurus had **4** super-sharp spikes on its tail end. These were **20 CENTIMETRES** longer than Stegosaurus's, at around **1 METRE**.

Human

Loricatisaurus

x3

Loricatosaurus relied on its scary-looking spikes to keep enemies away. It was slow and only ran at **16 KM/H**, which is just **3** times faster than humans walking.

Loricatosaurus had the longest dinosaur spikes, which were **3** times the size of the biggest T. rex teeth!

THE YOUNG ONES

What was life like for the young and baby dinosaurs millions of years ago? The stats and special numbers here will give you a few clues.

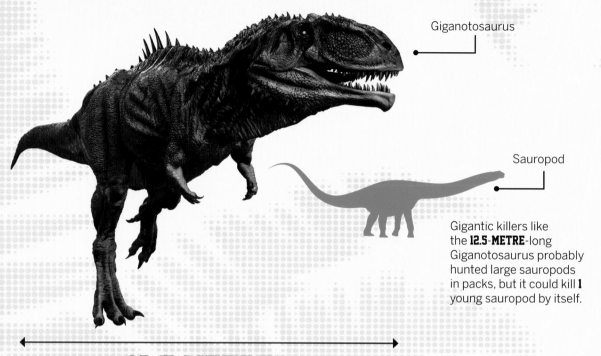

Giganotosaurus

Sauropod

Gigantic killers like the **12.5-METRE**-long Giganotosaurus probably hunted large sauropods in packs, but it could kill **1** young sauropod by itself.

12.5 METRES

As Tyrannosaurus rex became a teenager, it may have gained around **2 KILOGRAMS** a day. That's the weight of **5** baked bean cans.

Baked beans cans

NUMBER CRUNCH
The **20-METRE** Apatosaurus grew the most between the ages of **7** and **13**. It could have put on about **13 KILOGRAMS** every day.

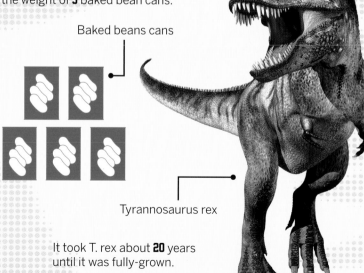

Tyrannosaurus rex

It took T. rex about **20** years until it was fully-grown.

When it was born, Diplodocus weighed as much as **8 KILOGRAMS**. That's heavier than **2** average newborn humans.

Newborn Diplodocus

Newborn humans

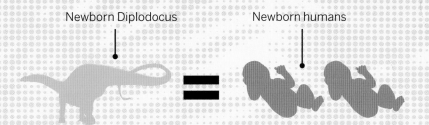

Young Maiasaura dinosaurs grew very quickly in the first **12 MONTHS**. They rocketed from **40 CENTIMETRES** to nearly **150 CENTIMETRES**.

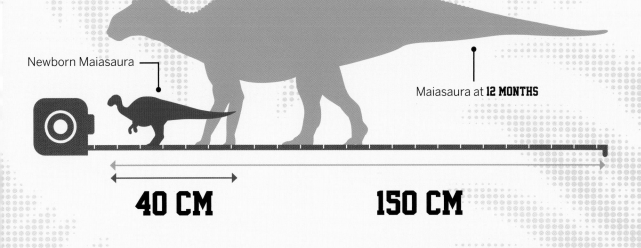

Newborn Maiasaura

Maiasaura at **12 MONTHS**

40 CM

150 CM

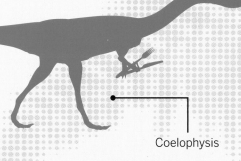

Human baby

Coelophysis

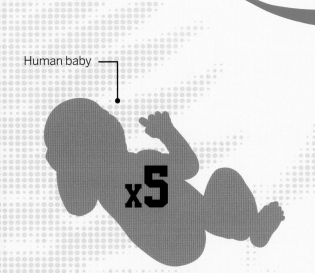

x5

Fossils found in **1947** of the **3-METRE**-long Coelophysis led scientists to believe it sometimes ate its own young because small bones were found in the creature's stomach. They now know it didn't because the reptiles in the stomach were actually a crocodile relative.

Some experts think young dinosaurs developed **5** times quicker than human babies.

STRANGE SIGHTS

No, your eyes aren't tricking you – these strange dinosaur details are all true and reveal what a crazy place planet Earth was millions of years ago.

Therizinosaurus

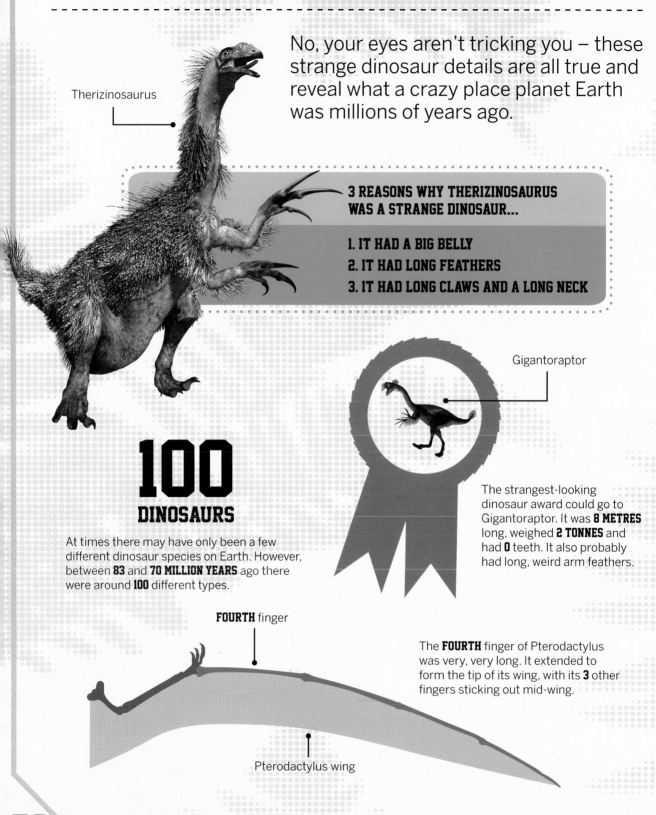

3 REASONS WHY THERIZINOSAURUS WAS A STRANGE DINOSAUR...

1. IT HAD A BIG BELLY
2. IT HAD LONG FEATHERS
3. IT HAD LONG CLAWS AND A LONG NECK

Gigantoraptor

100 DINOSAURS

At times there may have only been a few different dinosaur species on Earth. However, between **83** and **70 MILLION YEARS** ago there were around **100** different types.

The strangest-looking dinosaur award could go to Gigantoraptor. It was **8 METRES** long, weighed **2 TONNES** and had **0** teeth. It also probably had long, weird arm feathers.

FOURTH finger

The **FOURTH** finger of Pterodactylus was very, very long. It extended to form the tip of its wing, with its **3** other fingers sticking out mid-wing.

Pterodactylus wing

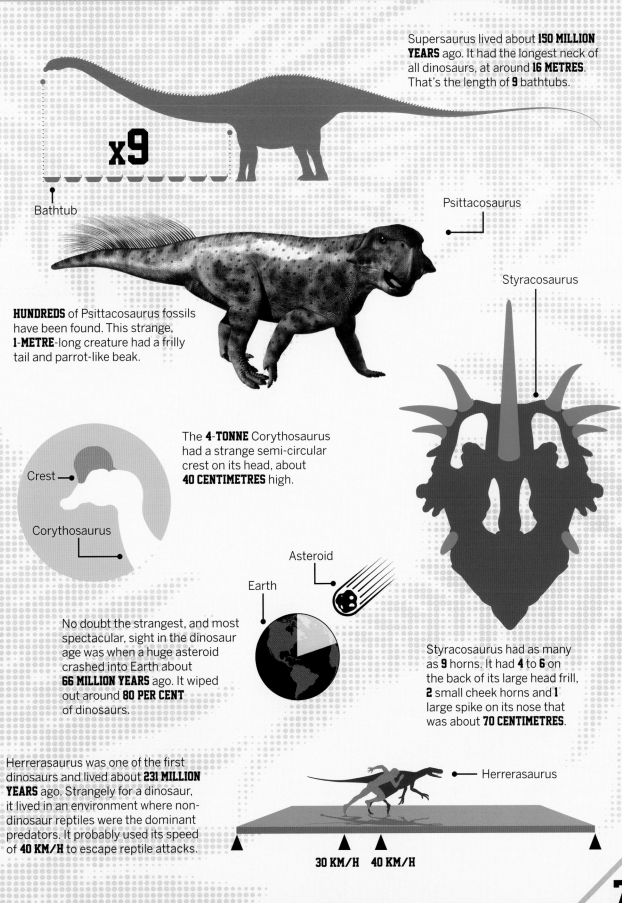

Supersaurus lived about **150 MILLION YEARS** ago. It had the longest neck of all dinosaurs, at around **16 METRES**. That's the length of **9** bathtubs.

x9

Bathtub

Psittacosaurus

Styracosaurus

HUNDREDS of Psittacosaurus fossils have been found. This strange, **1-METRE**-long creature had a frilly tail and parrot-like beak.

The **4-TONNE** Corythosaurus had a strange semi-circular crest on its head, about **40 CENTIMETRES** high.

Crest

Corythosaurus

Asteroid

Earth

No doubt the strangest, and most spectacular, sight in the dinosaur age was when a huge asteroid crashed into Earth about **66 MILLION YEARS** ago. It wiped out around **80 PER CENT** of dinosaurs.

Styracosaurus had as many as **9** horns. It had **4** to **6** on the back of its large head frill, **2** small cheek horns and **1** large spike on its nose that was about **70 CENTIMETRES**.

Herrerasaurus was one of the first dinosaurs and lived about **231 MILLION YEARS** ago. Strangely for a dinosaur, it lived in an environment where non-dinosaur reptiles were the dominant predators. It probably used its speed of **40 KM/H** to escape reptile attacks.

Herrerasaurus

30 KM/H   **40 KM/H**

FAMOUS FACES

You might recognise many of these dinosaur faces and names. Some of them are famous for fascinating reasons.

Edmontosaurus

Edmontosaurus is one of the most famous dinosaur heads. It had over **1000** teeth and stuffed plants and food in its cheeks.

Bony crest

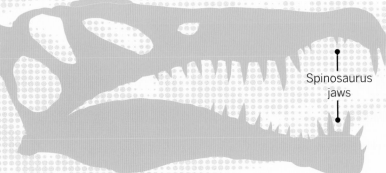

Spinosaurus jaws

As well as **1.7-METRE**-long jaws, Spinosaurus also had a small, bony crest above its eyes. This may have been brightly coloured to attract a mate.

Protoceratops

Velociraptor

NUMBER CRUNCH
Around **500** dinosaurs have been named in the last **20 YEARS**, including the **10-METRE**-long Torvosaurus. It may have been Europe's largest predator **150 MILLION YEARS** ago.

At **175 KILOGRAMS**, Protoceratops was **6** times heavier than Velociraptor, but they are **2** of the most famous battling dinosaurs. In **1971**, fossils of the rivals locked in a duel were found in the Gobi Desert, in Mongolia.

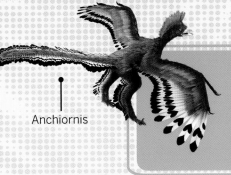

Anchiornis

The tiny feathered Anchiornis was only slightly longer than **2** pencils and it had interesting colouring...

ANCHIORNIS COLOURING

1. Bright red head crest
2. Grey body feathers
3. White leg feathers with black spots
4. White and black hand and arm feathers

Tyrannosaurus rex and the meat-eating Velociraptors starred in the **1993** blockbuster film *Jurassic Park*. The movie made over **$1 BILLION** at the cinema.

If Argentinosaurus lived in groups of **20**, for example, it means the herd's weight could have been heavier than **3** huge **BOEING 747** planes!

Zhuchengosaurus

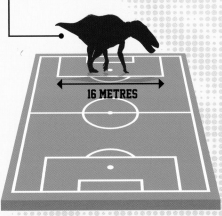

16 METRES

Archaeopteryx

Archaeopteryx lived **155** to **150 MILLION YEARS** ago. It's one of the most important fossils ever found and is the earliest bird species discovered.

Zhuchengosaurus was famous for being one of the biggest duckbill dinosaurs. It was **16 METRES** long – the width of a football pitch penalty area – and weighed **15 TONNES**.

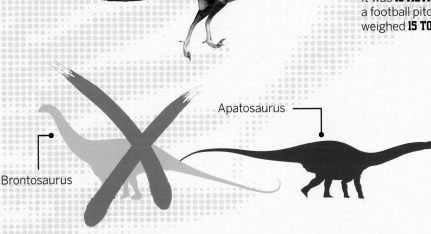

Apatosaurus

Brontosaurus

Apatosaurus is famous for being one of the biggest dinosaurs, at **20 TONNES** and up to **33 METRES**. But in the **20TH CENTURY**, its fossils were thought to be of another well-known heavyweight, the Brontosaurus.

MORE FAMOUS FACES

Triceratops may have been **300** times heavier than Velociraptor, but both of these famous creatures made big headlines **MILLIONS OF YEARS** ago…

Triceratops

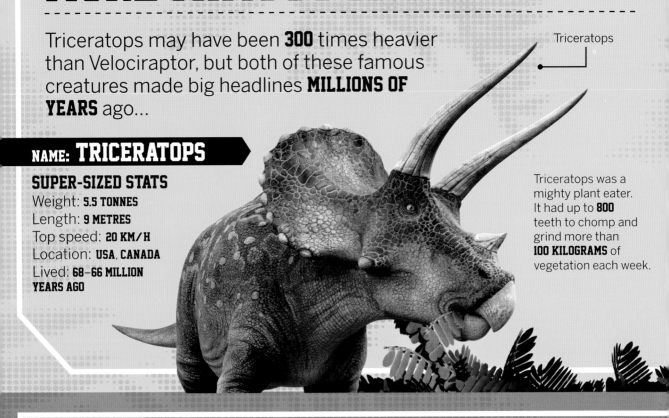

NAME: **TRICERATOPS**

SUPER-SIZED STATS
Weight: **5.5 TONNES**
Length: **9 METRES**
Top speed: **20 KM/H**
Location: **USA, CANADA**
Lived: **68–66 MILLION YEARS AGO**

Triceratops was a mighty plant eater. It had up to **800** teeth to chomp and grind more than **100 KILOGRAMS** of vegetation each week.

NAME: **VELOCIRAPTOR**

SUPER-SIZED STATS
Weight: **715 KILOGRAMS**
Length: **2 METRES**
Top speed: **40 KM/H**
Location: **MONGOLIA, CHINA, RUSSIA**
Lived: **75–71 MILLION YEARS AGO**

Velociraptor probably had hundreds of feathers on its body, but it had **ZERO** chance of flying – its feathers were too short for flight.

But compared to the length of its body, which at **2 METRES** was about the height of a very tall human, its arms were still longer than that of its distant cousin, T. rex.

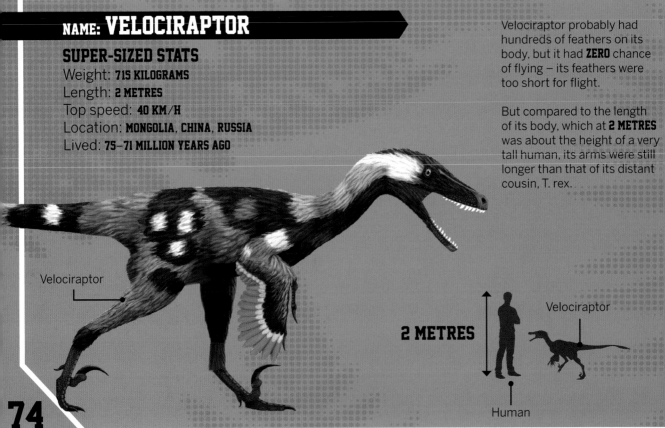

Velociraptor

2 METRES

Velociraptor

Human

THE NAME TRICERATOPSIS IS MADE OF 3 GREEK WORDS...

1. TRI = THREE
2. KERAS = HORN
3. OPS = FACE

Triceratops was among the last of the non-bird dinosaurs to roam the planet. It died out around **66 MILLION YEARS** ago.

x3

The famous Triceratops looked like a modern rhino, but it was about **2.5** times heavier. It was also the length of **3** Bengal tigers.

R.I.P
TRICERATOPS

Triceratops comes from a distinct group of dinos called ceratopsians. Some had **3** head spikes like Triceratops, while others had **2, 1** or **0**.

x3 BENGAL TIGERS

VELOCIRAPTOR WASN'T A FUSSY EATER. IT HUNTED AND SCAVENGED LOTS OF FOOD SOURCES INCLUDING...

1. Lizards
2. Dead remains
3. Small dinosaurs
4. Eggs
5. Mammals

Some scientists think Velociraptor could have reached speeds of **60 KM/H** in short bursts.

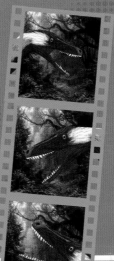

T. rex wasn't the only movie star. The vicious Velociraptor also shot to fame after being depicted in *Jurassic Park* in the **1990s**.

NUMBER CRUNCH
Experts think that Velociraptor had a large skull for its small size. Its skull could have been **23 CENTIMETRES** long, which is almost the height its hips were from the ground.

THE BRAIN GAME

You'll need some quick thinking to take in all these brain-busting facts and stats about smart, and not so smart, dinosaurs!

2.5 METRES

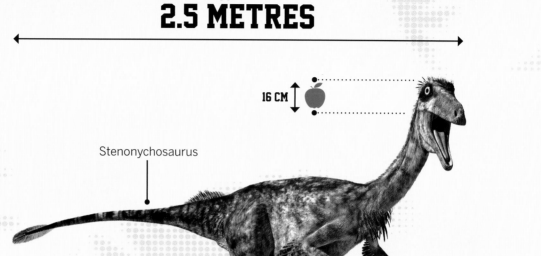

16 CM

Stenonychosaurus

The **2.5-METRE**-long predator Stenonychosaurus is said to have had the biggest brain in relation to body size. Its brain was about **16 CENTIMETRES**, which is the size of a very small apple! That might not sound big, but it is big for a dinosaur!

Stenonychosaurus managed to survive for **5 MILLION YEARS**, but it was probably only about as clever as a modern chicken.

Omeisaurus

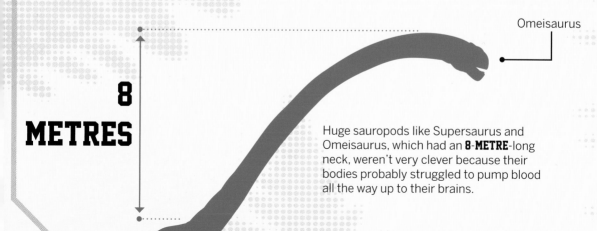

8 METRES

Huge sauropods like Supersaurus and Omeisaurus, which had an **8-METRE**-long neck, weren't very clever because their bodies probably struggled to pump blood all the way up to their brains.

Despite being **7 METRES** long, which is about the length of a minibus, the brain of a Stegosaurus was **25** times smaller than that of an adult human's.

Stegosaurus brain

Human brain

x25 SMALLER

Stegosaurus

5-cent coin (actual size)

The part of the brain it used for thinking was only about the size of a **5**-cent coin.

Experts used to think Stegosaurus may have had **2** brains, with a second in its spine. They now know that's not true.

The **6-TONNE** armoured Ankylosaurus had a small brain for its size and used muscle power, rather than brain power, to defend itself.

Ankylosaurus

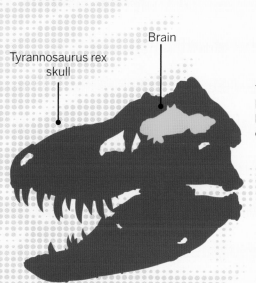

Brain

Tyrannosaurus rex skull

Tyrannosaurus rex and other large predators needed clever brains for **1** reason – they had to outsmart the dinosaurs they hunted.

3 THINGS THAT CAN HELP MAKE A DINOSAUR SMARTER...

1. Forward-facing eyes
2. Hunting and living in packs
3. Having digits, like fingers, on their hands

CRAZY CLAWS

From sharp brains to even sharper claws, it's time to take a look at dinosaurs that were a cut above the rest millions of years ago.

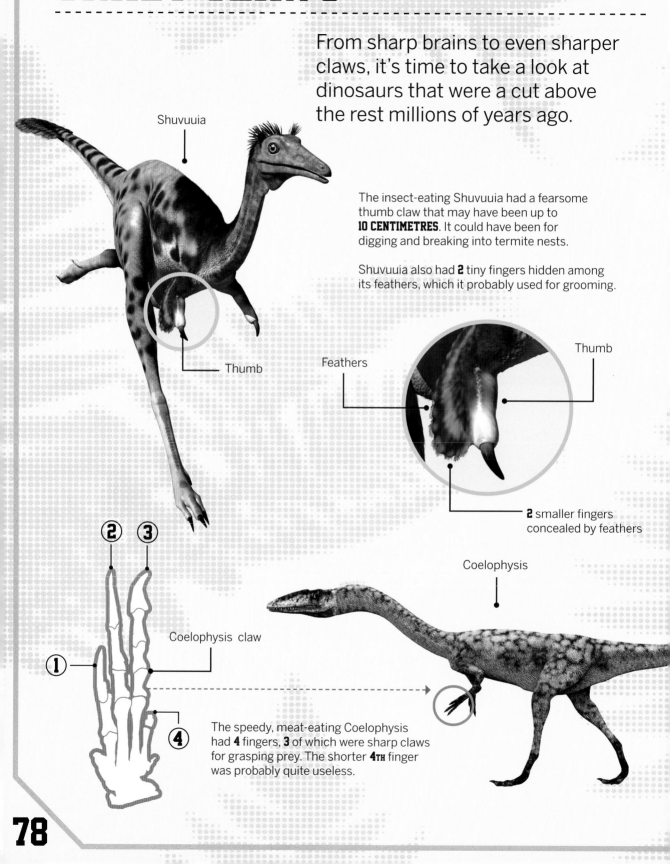

Shuvuuia

The insect-eating Shuvuuia had a fearsome thumb claw that may have been up to **10 CENTIMETRES**. It could have been for digging and breaking into termite nests.

Shuvuuia also had **2** tiny fingers hidden among its feathers, which it probably used for grooming.

Thumb

Feathers

Thumb

2 smaller fingers concealed by feathers

Coelophysis

② ③

Coelophysis claw

① ④

The speedy, meat-eating Coelophysis had **4** fingers, **3** of which were sharp claws for grasping prey. The shorter **4TH** finger was probably quite useless.

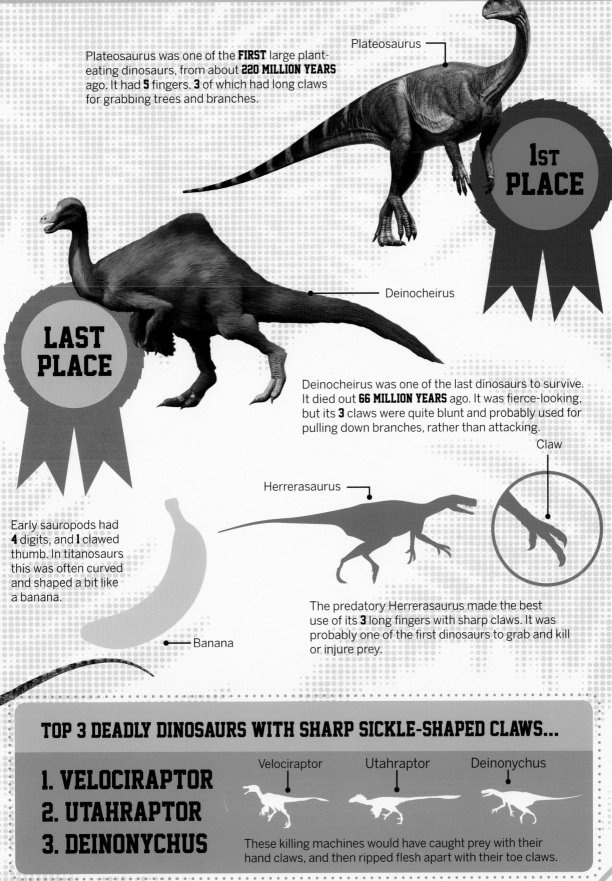

Plateosaurus was one of the **FIRST** large plant-eating dinosaurs, from about **220 MILLION YEARS** ago. It had **5** fingers, **3** of which had long claws for grabbing trees and branches.

Plateosaurus

1ST PLACE

Deinocheirus

LAST PLACE

Deinocheirus was one of the last dinosaurs to survive. It died out **66 MILLION YEARS** ago. It was fierce-looking, but its **3** claws were quite blunt and probably used for pulling down branches, rather than attacking.

Claw

Herrerasaurus

Early sauropods had **4** digits, and **1** clawed thumb. In titanosaurs this was often curved and shaped a bit like a banana.

Banana

The predatory Herrerasaurus made the best use of its **3** long fingers with sharp claws. It was probably one of the first dinosaurs to grab and kill or injure prey.

TOP 3 DEADLY DINOSAURS WITH SHARP SICKLE-SHAPED CLAWS...

1. VELOCIRAPTOR
2. UTAHRAPTOR
3. DEINONYCHUS

Velociraptor

Utahraptor

Deinonychus

These killing machines would have caught prey with their hand claws, and then ripped flesh apart with their toe claws.

79

LOOKING SHARP

Therizinosaurus and Megaraptor had the most amazing dinosaur claws ever discovered. They were big, brutal and could bash most attackers away with a single swipe!

Therizinosaurus

NAME: **THERIZINOSAURUS**

SUPER-SIZED STATS
Weight: **5 TONNES**
Length: **8–10 METRES**
Top speed: **32 KM/H**
Location: **MONGOLIA**
Lived: **70–65 MILLION YEARS AGO**

NAME: **MEGARAPTOR**

SUPER-SIZED STATS
Weight: **1 TONNE**
Length: **8 METRES**
Top speed: **OVER 40 KM/H**
Location: **SOUTH AMERICA**
Lived: **90–85 MILLION YEARS AGO**

Megaraptor

Therizinosaurus had the longest claws of any animal... ever! Its largest claw was at least **70 CENTIMETRES**, which is nearly **8** times longer than a Velociraptor's lethal toe claw.

Some scientists believe that the claws could have been nearly **1 METRE** because they were also covered in a horny coating. That's **100** times bigger than a human fingernail.

Giraffe

Therizinosaurus claw

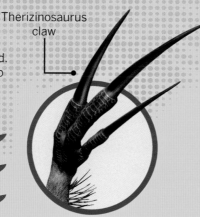

Therizinosaurus had **3** fearsome claws on each hand. They acted like **6** super-sharp swords and would have scared mighty predators like Tarbosaurus.

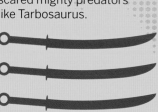

At nearly **10 METRES** long and weighing **5 TONNES**, Therizinosaurus would have towered over a giraffe.

Megaraptor had **3** claws on each of its hands. Its largest claw was an impressive **40 CENTIMETRES** – about the length of **2** human hands.

40 CM

Claw

When Megaraptor remains were first discovered in the **1990s**, it was thought that its giant hand claw was actually the dinosaur's foot.

Pointy weapon

3 REASONS WHY MEGARAPTOR WAS A FIERCE FIGHTER...

1. Killing claws to slash prey
2. Light, lean and quick
3. Powerful jaws and razor-sharp teeth

Megaraptor probably used its **2** pointy weapons to prey on Austroraptors, which were about a **QUARTER** of its size and would have made a very tasty meal.

NORTH VERSUS SOUTH

Let's go from one dinosaur extreme to the other and discover all about the most northerly, and most southerly, dinosaurs that we know of.

Stenonychosaurus

Remains of Stenonychosaurus have been found in Alaska, in the Arctic Circle, making it the most northerly dinosaur discovered.

N

W

E

S

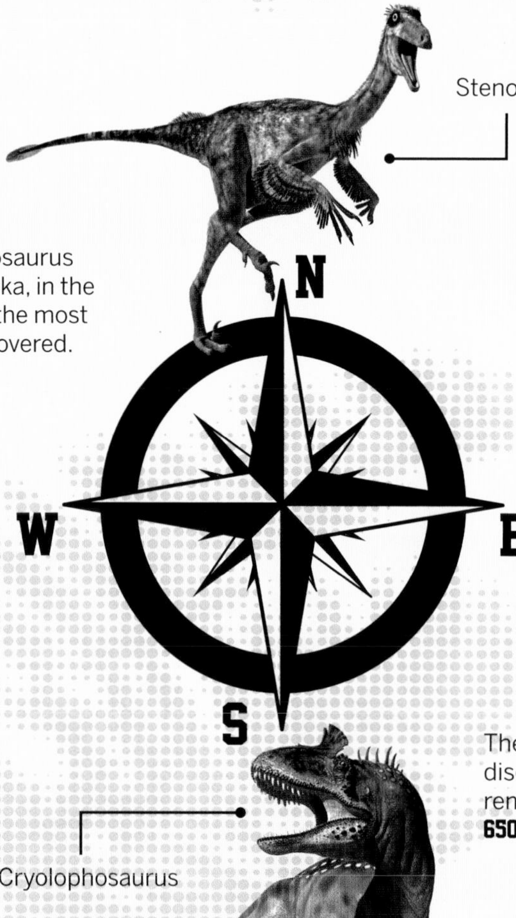

The most southerly dinosaur discovered is Cryolophosaurus. Its remains were found in Antarctica, just **650 KILOMETRES** from the South Pole.

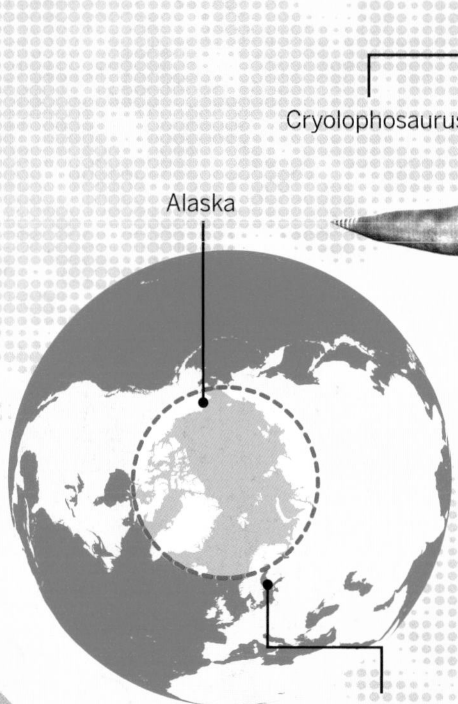

Cryolophosaurus

Alaska

Arctic circle

Antarctica

Cryolophosaurus remains were unearthed in **1991**, making it the **FIRST** theropod found in Antarctica.

The American team that made the discovery went back to the same spot **13 YEARS** later and found even more remains.

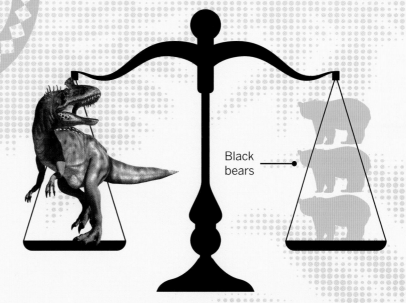

Cryolophosaurus was the most fearsome killer on the continent **183 MILLION YEARS** ago, but it was still only **HALF** the length of a T. rex.

It weighed as much as **3** American black bears.

Black bears

5 PER CENT

That's how much of the cold Antarctic landscape scientists can search for dinosaurs. Most of the Antarctic is buried in sea or ice.

Temperatures were warmer at the Poles than they are now, but could still be below **0°C** at times. Stenonychosaurus was probably covered in short feathers to keep warm.

NUMBER CRUNCH
Because of the harsh conditions in the Arctic Circle, some experts think that lots of dinosaurs in this region died before they reached **20 YEARS** old.

Troodon would have lived for months at a time in winter darkness in the Arctic Circle. It had **4** main weapons to catch prey under the moonlight...

1. Sharp claws
2. Good eyesight
3. Great speed
4. Clever brain

BRILL BONES & FAB FOSSILS

Everything dinosaur experts know comes from the fossils (preserved remains) found in rocks and under the ground. Dig around these pages to see what else you can learn...

In **2003**, in east Asia, an amazing adult Psittacosaurus fossil was discovered lying next to a record-breaking **34** babies. This suggests a close relationship between the parent and its young.

x34

Stenonychosaurus eye

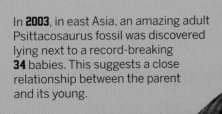

4.5 CM

No one knows the colour of the huge **4.5-CENTIMETRE**-wide eyeballs of Stenonychosaurus. Hardly any fossilized dinosaur eyeballs exist, but other animal hunters with good vision, such as owls, often have yellow eyes.

NUMBER CRUNCH

Leaellynasaura was smaller than an average **10**-year-old child, but its amazing **3-METRE**-long tail had over **70** bones.

Loricatosaurus

The fossil remains of sharp body spikes from the **2-TONNE** Loricatosaurus may have been **TWICE** as long when the creature was alive. This is because the bones were covered by a tough, horny sheath that was continually growing, but it doesn't survive in fossils.

1,000,000 years

That's the minimum time it usually takes for fossil remains to form into solid rock. Some dinosaur fossils are over **200 MILLION YEARS** old.

Germany

Stegosaurus hand

12 fossils of the bird Archaeopteryx have been found in southern Germany. They are over **150 MILLION YEARS** old and show that modern birds evolved from small, predatory dinosaurs.

⑤

④

③

②

①

Stegosaurus needed strong hands and legs to support its **3-TONNE** weight. Its skeletal remains show it had **5** fingers on each hand.

The Nemegt Formation is a large area in Mongolia where fossils of **25** dinosaurs have been found. In the **1950s**, bulldozers and explosives were used to extract the fossil remains out of the ancient rocks.

100%

Amazingly, an ichthyosaur fossil found in Lyme Regis, southern England, had every bone in place. These reptiles have been found in rocks there since the **19TH CENTURY**.

MORE BRILL BONES & FAB FOSSILS

15,000 KM

Fossils of a meat eater called Syntarsus were found in South Africa and in Arizona. That's a distance of **15,000 KILOMETRES**, which suggests Syntarsus travelled right across the huge Pangaea continent about **188 MILLION YEARS** ago.

TITANOSAUR REMAINS FOUND IN PATAGONIA ARGENTINA, IN THE 21ST CENTURY

223 bones belonging to the titanosaur group
18 months to excavate
7 expeditions to the fossil site by experts

A **37-METRE**-long titanosaur is on display at the American Museum of Natural History in New York, made with copies of the giant bones found at the Argentinian excavation site. It's so big the head pokes into another room!

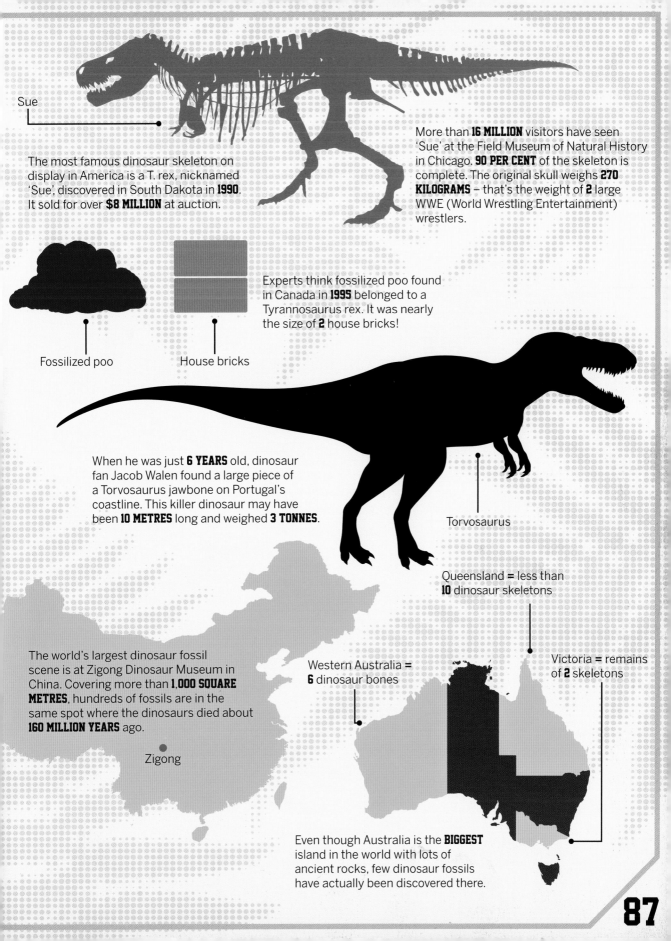

Sue

The most famous dinosaur skeleton on display in America is a T. rex, nicknamed 'Sue', discovered in South Dakota in **1990**. It sold for over **$8 MILLION** at auction.

More than **16 MILLION** visitors have seen 'Sue' at the Field Museum of Natural History in Chicago. **90 PER CENT** of the skeleton is complete. The original skull weighs **270 KILOGRAMS** – that's the weight of **2** large WWE (World Wrestling Entertainment) wrestlers.

Experts think fossilized poo found in Canada in **1995** belonged to a Tyrannosaurus rex. It was nearly the size of **2** house bricks!

Fossilized poo

House bricks

When he was just **6 YEARS** old, dinosaur fan Jacob Walen found a large piece of a Torvosaurus jawbone on Portugal's coastline. This killer dinosaur may have been **10 METRES** long and weighed **3 TONNES**.

Torvosaurus

Queensland = less than **10** dinosaur skeletons

The world's largest dinosaur fossil scene is at Zigong Dinosaur Museum in China. Covering more than **1,000 SQUARE METRES**, hundreds of fossils are in the same spot where the dinosaurs died about **160 MILLION YEARS** ago.

Western Australia = **6** dinosaur bones

Victoria = remains of **2** skeletons

Zigong

Even though Australia is the **BIGGEST** island in the world with lots of ancient rocks, few dinosaur fossils have actually been discovered there.

EGG-CITING FACTS

Dinosaur eggs can reveal a lot about dinosaurs, sometimes more than even bones and fossils can. These numbers and facts will help you learn even more about the ancient creatures that once ruled the Earth.

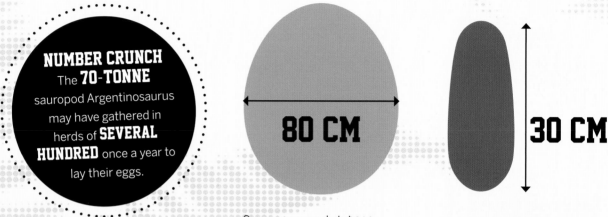

NUMBER CRUNCH The **70-TONNE** sauropod Argentinosaurus may have gathered in herds of **SEVERAL HUNDRED** once a year to lay their eggs.

80 CM

30 CM

Super sauropod stats: Oval-shaped eggs up to **80 CENTIMETRES** in circumference.

Top tyrannosaur trivia: Thinner, oval-shaped eggs, around **30 CENTIMETRES** long.

x200

More than **200** Maiasaura fossils were discovered in Montana, USA, in **1978**. Many were eggs and babies, and experts called the area 'Egg Mountain'.

Maiasaura laid eggs in a huge nest built on the ground. Its eggs may have been **1 METRE** high and **2 METRES** wide, which is bigger than the average dining table.

1 METRE

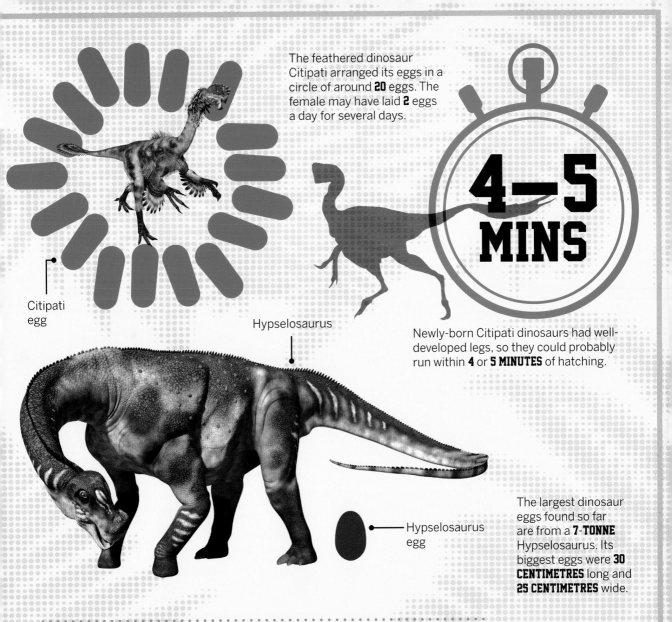

The feathered dinosaur Citipati arranged its eggs in a circle of around **20** eggs. The female may have laid **2** eggs a day for several days.

Citipati egg

Hypselosaurus

4–5 MINS

Newly-born Citipati dinosaurs had well-developed legs, so they could probably run within **4** or **5 MINUTES** of hatching.

Hypselosaurus egg

The largest dinosaur eggs found so far are from a **7-TONNE** Hypselosaurus. Its biggest eggs were **30 CENTIMETRES** long and **25 CENTIMETRES** wide.

TOP 3 LARGEST DINOSAUR EGGS DISCOVERED

1. Hypselosaurus = equivalent to **73** chicken eggs

2. Macroelongatoolithus = equivalent to **70** chicken eggs

3. Hypacrosaurus = equivalent to **65** chicken eggs

MORE EGG-CITING FACTS

The eggs found in the biggest dinosaur nest have a name of their own – Macroelongatoolithus. They were about **30 CENTIMETRES** long and **28** eggs were found in **1** nest in China.

x28

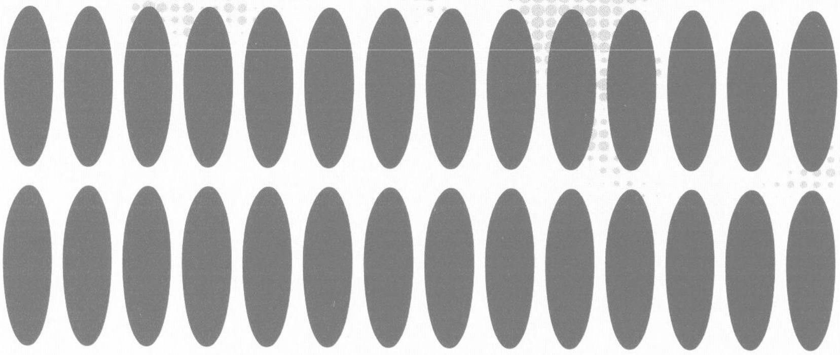

The giant nest was **3 METRES** wide, which is the length of **2** pool cues.

Pool cues

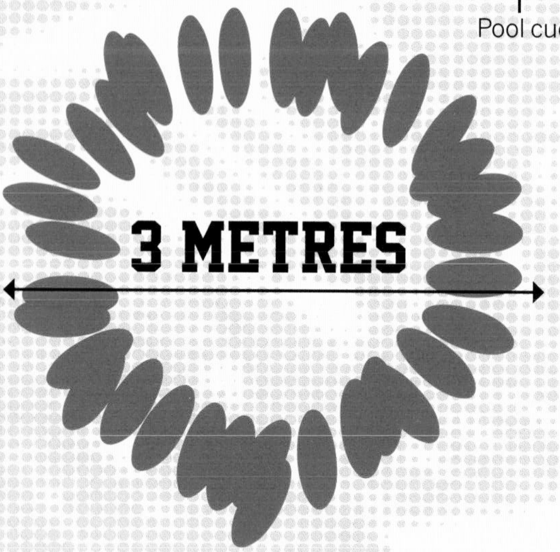

3 METRES

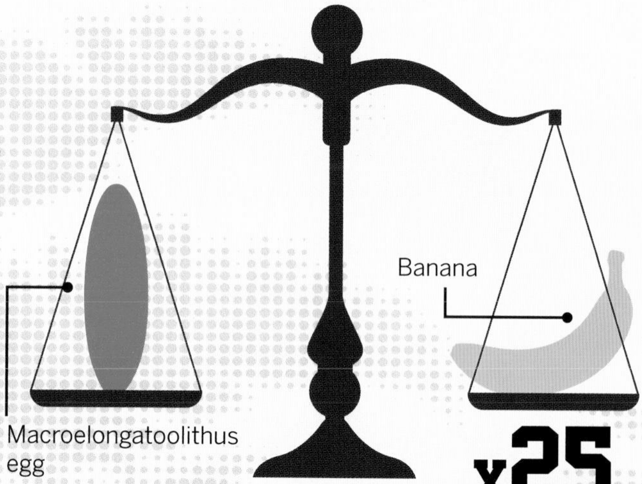

Macroelongatoolithus egg

Banana

x25

The eggs were around **5 KILOGRAMS** and equal in weight to **25 BANANAS**.

Gigantoraptor

The dinosaur thought to have laid the Macroelongatoolithus eggs was the **8-METRE**-long Gigantoraptor, but no one knows for certain.

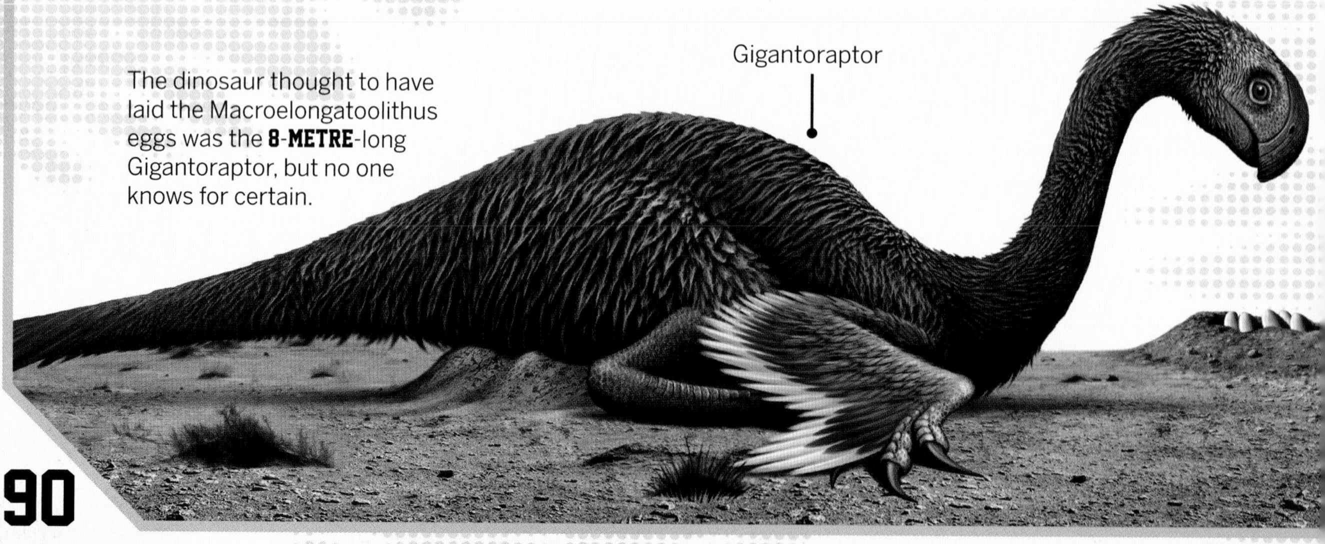

Stenonychosaurus could have laid up to **24** eggs in its nest. It probably used snout to crack open and eat other dinosaurs' eggs.

Stenonychosaurus

x24

Oviraptor

Fossilized dinosaur eggs are very rare, but they have still been found at over **200** sites around the world.

200

In the early **20TH CENTURY**, scientists thought Oviraptor stole other eggs, but they now know it didn't. Unfairly, the word 'Oviraptor' means 'egg thief' in Greek.

NOT GUILTY!

18 METRES

Camarasaurus

Ichthyosaurs, like the gigantic **21-METRE** Shastasurus reptile, laid **0** eggs. That's because they were adapted to sea life and gave birth to live young in the water.

Shastasaurus

The sauropod Camarasaurus was around **18 METRES** as an adult, but its babies measured just **1 METRE** curled up inside their egg.

Camarasaurus egg

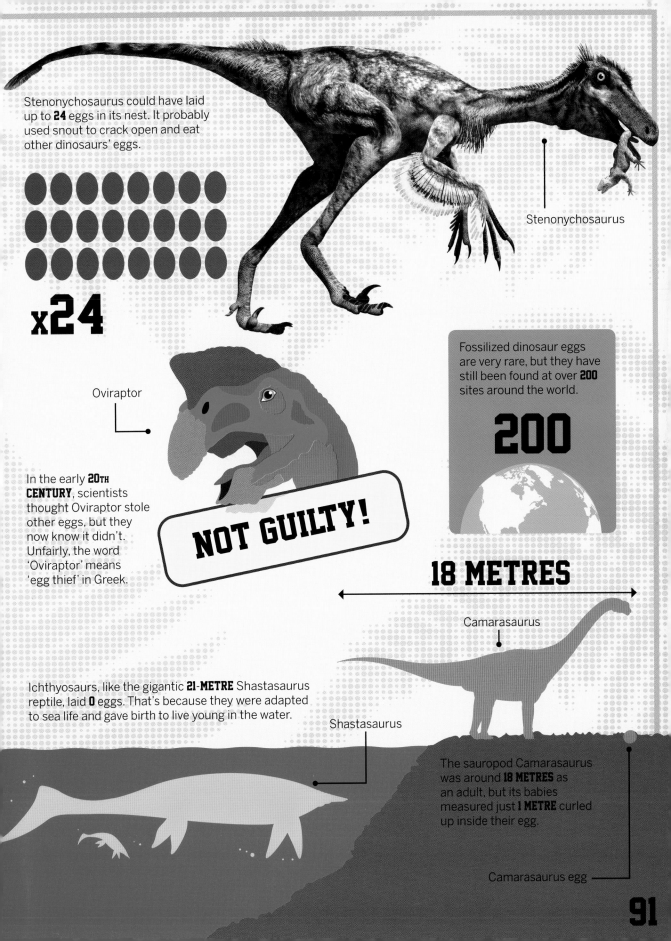

EPIC EXTINCTION

When a mighty asteroid struck planet Earth, it signaled the end of the dinosaurs' reign. Some of the most amazing, ancient, fearsome and fascinating creatures would soon die out for ever.

Most experts agree that the dinosaurs began to die out **66 MILLION** years ago. This was when a huge asteroid struck the Earth, **29 KILOMETRES** off the coast of what is now Mexico.

The asteroid crater made by its impact wasn't discovered until **1990**. The ferocious flying object was **11 KILOMETRES** wide – that's **25** times bigger than the Empire State Building in New York.

X25

Empire State Building

Asteroid

The crater was **180 KILOMETRES** across. That's more than the distance between New York and Philadelphia.

7,000 KM/H   **100,000 KM/H**

The giant rock could have been travelling at **100,000 KILOMETRES** an hour. The fastest fighter jets only reach around **7,000 KILOMETRES** per hour.

Atomic bomb

It struck Earth with a force **2 MILLION** times stronger than an atomic bomb. Some experts think it could even have been **10 BILLION** times stronger.

10,000°C
The meteorite caused a radiation fireball of **10,000°C**. Anything within **600 MILES** of the impact was sizzled in minutes.

TOP 5 THINGS THE ASTEROID CRASH CREATED THAT BEGAN TO KILL OFF DINOSAURS

1. POISONOUS GASES IN THE AIR
2. BLOCKING OF SUNLIGHT
3. HUGE FIRES
4. EARTHQUAKES
5. TSUNAMIS

In India, about **15,000 KILOMETRES** away from the meteorite impact, massive volcanic eruptions made conditions even worse for dinosaurs on Earth.

85 PER CENT
That's the percentage of living things, including dinosaurs, that could have been killed because of the asteroid impact.

There have been **5** mass extinctions that nearly wiped out all life on Earth. The **5TH**, at the end of the Cretaceous period **66 MILLION YEARS** ago, killed off the dinosaurs.

DINOSAUR NUMBER CRUNCH QUICK QUIZ

You'll find the answers to all these number crunch questions lurking somewhere in this book, but don't cheat – see how many you can answer without looking!

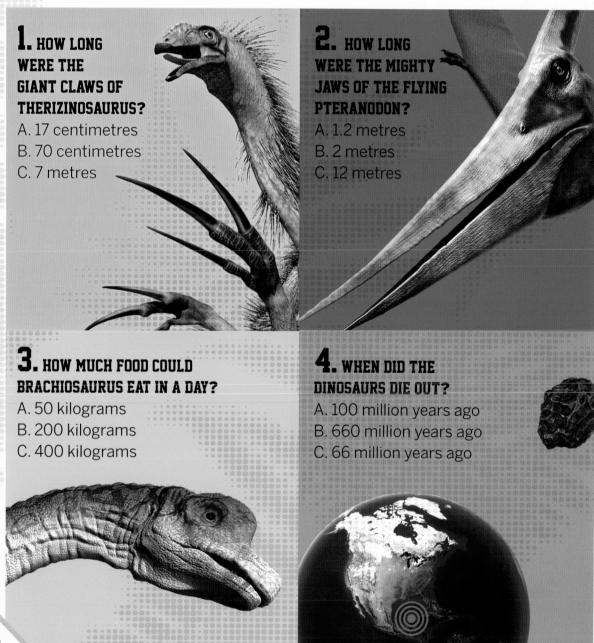

1. HOW LONG WERE THE GIANT CLAWS OF THERIZINOSAURUS?
A. 17 centimetres
B. 70 centimetres
C. 7 metres

2. HOW LONG WERE THE MIGHTY JAWS OF THE FLYING PTERANODON?
A. 1.2 metres
B. 2 metres
C. 12 metres

3. HOW MUCH FOOD COULD BRACHIOSAURUS EAT IN A DAY?
A. 50 kilograms
B. 200 kilograms
C. 400 kilograms

4. WHEN DID THE DINOSAURS DIE OUT?
A. 100 million years ago
B. 660 million years ago
C. 66 million years ago

5. HOW MANY SPIKES DID PACHYCEPHALOSAURUS HAVE?

A. 5
B. 3
C. Loads

6. A TYRANNOSAURUS REX'S BITE WAS MORE POWERFUL THAN AN ALLIGATOR'S BUT BY HOW MANY TIMES?

A. 6 times
B. 2 times
C. 10 times

7. HOW LONG WAS THE TAIL OF A DIPLODOCUS?

A. 1.4 metres
B. 14 metres
C. 140 metres

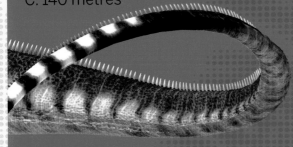

8. HOW MANY SHARP NECK SPIKES DID AMARGASAURUS HAVE?

A. 18
B. 40
C. 1

9. WHAT WAS THE WINGSPAN OF THE FLYING REPTILE QUETZALCOATLUS?

A. 1 metre
B. 8 metres
C. 11 metres

10. DEINOCHEIRUS WAS THE TALLEST THEROPOD, BUT HOW HIGH COULD IT REACH?

A. 1.5 metres
B. 5 metres
C. 50 metres

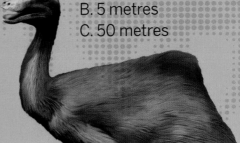

PICTURE CREDITS

The publishers would like to thank the following sources for their kind permission to reproduce the pictures in this book.

All images © Carlton Books except the following:

Page 6: DM7/Shutterstock; 8C: Catmando/Shutterstock; 9R: Sergey Novikov/Shutterstock; 14: Herschel Hoffmeyer/Shutterstock; 15: Warpaint/Shutterstock; 17BC: Andrea Crisante/Shutterstock; 17BR: Herschel Hoffmeyer/Shutterstock; 19C: Elena Duvernay/Stocktrek Images/Alamy Stock Photo; 23: Science Photo Library/Alamy Stock Photo; 24B: Warpaint/Shutterstock; 31R: Elena Duvernay/Stocktrek Images/Alamy Stock Photo; 32B: Robert Fabiani Jr.; 36BR: DM7/Shutterstock; 37: Corey Ford/Stocktrek Images/Alamy Stock Photo; 43T: Science Photo Library/Alamy Stock Photo; 44T: DK Images; 45BL: Jose Antonio Penas/Science Photo Library; 46T: Catmando/Shutterstock; 49R: Cetus/Shutterstock; 51C: Catmando/Shutterstock; 52: Bob Orsillo/Shutterstock; 58T: Nobumichi Tamura/Stocktrek/Alamy Stock Photo; 60R: Herschel Hoffmeyer/Shutterstock; 65C: Herschel Hoffmeyer/Shutterstock; 65L: Bob Orsillo/Shutterstock; 65C: Herschel Hoffmeyer/Shutterstock; 68T: Herschel Hoffmeyer/Shutterstock; 70R: Valentyna Chukhlyebova/Alamy Stock Photo; 72BL: Jose Antonio Penas/Science Photo Library; 74BL: Scott Hartman; 74B: Scott Hartman; 77L: Fat Jackey/Shutterstock; 78BR: Michael Rosskothen/Shutterstock; 79L: Nobumichi Tamura/Stocktrek/Alamy Stock Photo; 80B: Herschel Hoffmeyer/Shutterstock; 90: Mohamad Haghani/Stocktrek/Alamy Stock Photo; 95BR: Nobumichi Tamura/Stocktrek/Alamy Stock Photo

Every effort has been made to acknowledge correctly and contact the source and/or copyright holder of each picture and Carlton Books Limited apologises for any unintentional errors or omissions that will be corrected in future editions of this book.